First published in the United Kingdom in 2018 by
Pavilion
43 Great Ormond Street
London WC1N 3HZ

ISBN 978-1-91162-401-1

A CIP catalogue record for this book is available from the British
Library

10 9 8 7 6 5 4 3 2

Reproduction by Mission, Hong Kong
Printed and bound by Imak Ofset, Turkey

This book can be ordered direct from the publisher at
www.pavilionbooks.com

Neither the author nor the publisher can accept responsibility
for any injury or illness that may arise as a result of following the
advice contained in this work. Any application of the information
contained in the book is at the reader's sole discretion.

MOB
KITCHEN

BEN LEBUS

PAVILION

INTRODUCING... 6

INTRODUCING...

What's up MOB! Welcome to the first MOB Kitchen book, jammed full of big cheap meals packed with vibrant flavours, using the freshest ingredients with delicious results. Having provided the online space that was so desperately needed by students and young professionals, we are now bringing this into the real world. This book is the ultimate affordable cooking bible – you're gonna absolutely love it!

I have always adored food. It is the first thing I think about when I wake up, and the last thing I think about before I go to sleep. When I was much younger, I would often cook dinner for my brothers and my parents. I loved whacking a bunch of fresh ingredients in a bowl and creating a really simple, delicious salad. I would always try out different pasta sauces or experiment with the Sunday roast while singing along to my favourite Van Morrison tunes.

When I moved into my first house with my four best mates at university, I relished the opportunity to cook in my own kitchen. However, I quickly saw that this enthusiasm was not shared by my friends. The boys, Paddy and Chester, would cook bacon sarnies and pesto pasta five nights a week. The rest of the time they would buy a ready-made soup from the local shop. I didn't get it. I didn't understand why they lacked the confidence in the kitchen to cook a proper meal.

Something needed to be done. I wanted to prove that you didn't have to be rich or talented to cook a healthy, delicious meal. So I started to write a blog with a series of recipes that would feed us all for under a tenner. In my final year at university, I filmed 20 of the recipes to share online. I came up with the name MOB Kitchen and launched the channel in August 2016.

So, what exactly is MOB Kitchen? When I was at university, young people weren't cooking. The phrases 'I can't be bothered' or 'It's too expensive' were commonplace in the student kitchen. Across the social media sites on which we spent all of our time, there were no relevant or accessible videos showing us that cooking healthy, delicious food is easy, fun and affordable. We needed a site to show us that by using simple, everyday ingredients in the right way, we could cook for our housemates, colleagues and friends without any fuss. Before MOB Kitchen, this simply did not exist. With real prices, real food, real imperfections and real music, MOB Kitchen provided the answer. MOB Kitchen is a movement away from the take-away, away from processed food, and back into the kitchen. Thousands of students, young professionals and families across the country cook the recipes every week, which is why it is time to present to you the first MOB Kitchen cookbook.

How is the book different? Well, firstly, we have a unique approach to our budgeting and pricing. All we assume is that you have salt, pepper and olive oil in your kitchen. As a student I hated it when recipes assumed I had certain things in my kitchen. In reality, all I had in my cupboards was some old electricity bills and lots of mouldy apples. MOB Kitchen does not assume you have the odd dusting of cumin on one shelf and the perfect number of bay leaves on another. Most people shop day-to-day, thinking only one or two meals in advance. So, for every recipe in this book, all we expect is that you have these three kitchen staples. Nothing more. So call up your friends, pick whichever recipe you would like to cook and get on it.

I have split the book into six chapters, starting with Brunch MOB, which brings fresh, unique recipes to the breakfast game. You'll no longer be limited to scrambled eggs and baked beans – these recipes are mind blowing. Second up is Fresh MOB, full of simple salads, soups and some banging veggie feasts bursting with flavour. Numero three is Speedy MOB. All the recipes take 30 minutes or less, no skill is needed and they're perfect for lunches or quick suppers. Next we have Fuss-free MOB. At uni it was such a pain washing up loads of dishes after a big dinner, so ALL of these recipes are one-dish wonders. Easy as 1, 2, 3. The fifth chapter is Flashy MOB. These recipes are a bit more involved, great for a weekend dinner party. So get your MOB over and show them your skills. The final chapter is Fakeaway MOB, featuring recipes for fast food that you thought you could only buy at the local babby, but you can actually do at home. AND, they are much fresher, much cheaper and much more delicious!

The music side. For me, music is a key part of cooking. I love blaring tunes in the kitchen and singing along while I cook. When I created the first series of videos, I decided to go against the usual food video trends and sacked off using boring lift music. I approached my friends in bands and asked them if they would let me use some of their tracks. They said yes, and it just worked. The videos were so much more upbeat and relatable. I also created a series of playlists for people to follow and listen to while they were cooking the recipes at home.

This book is the culmination of a MOB movement that has been building since we started. We are the MOB. We are the students and young professionals. The families. We don't have a lot of cash to spare. But we want to cook good food. We want to eat delicious dinners. We don't want to be told that all we can cook is marmite spaghetti and baked beans on toast. We want restaurant-quality munch in our own homes. And MOB Kitchen is the answer.

Big love MOB, Ben

KEY TO SYMBOLS

[★] MOB classic (one of the best-loved recipes from the channel)
[V] Vegetarian
[VG] Vegan

When you see one of the following Spotify Codes, you can scan it using the Spotify app to listen to the corresponding playlist/song.

Open ⬢ | Search Q | Scan ⬚

1

BRUNCH MOB

INGREDIENTS

4 sweet potatoes
11 eggs
fresh parsley
spring onions (scallions)
dried chilli flakes
2 large avocados
fresh chives
1 lemon
salt and pepper
olive oil

THE SOFT EGG. THE SOFT GUAC. THE CRISPY RÖSTI. A TEXTURE MATCH MADE IN HEAVEN.

THE CRISPIEST SWEET POTATO RÖSTI WITH POACHED EGGS & GUAC [★]

01 Preheat the oven to 180°C fan (200°C/400°F/Gas Mark 6).

02 Peel and grate the sweet potatoes with a normal box grater.

03 Add the grated potato into a bowl. Crack in 3 eggs. Add a handful of chopped parsley, a handful of chopped spring onions and 1 teaspoon of dried chilli flakes. Season with salt, pepper and olive oil. Mix everything together.

04 Get a baking sheet. Line it with baking paper. Make 8 fishcake-sized röstis, and line them up on the sheet. They will be quite loose at this point, but don't worry. Just squeeze them into shape and whack in the oven. They will firm up and crisp up. Bake for 30 minutes, turning after 20 minutes.

05 Guac time. Scoop the flesh out of the avocados and mash it in a bowl. Add a handful of chopped chives and the juice of a lemon, and season with salt, pepper and olive oil. Mash everything together and set aside.

06 Egg time. Boil a pan of water. Carefully crack 2 eggs into separate glasses. With a fork or a whisk, create a little whirlpool in the water. Pour the eggs into the water, not in the centre of the whirlpool, but on the edge. The water will fold the white over the yolk and should form a nice little ball.

07 Cook for 3 minutes on a medium heat. To check if they're done, just gently lift the egg with a spoon. If the white is still a bit wobbly, leave it for 10 more seconds. If it's firm, remove from the heat. Repeat for the remaining 6 eggs. It might be quicker to get two pans going simultaneously!

08 Assembly time. Spoon a good helping of guac on top of the rösti. And then put your egg on top. Allow 2 röstis and 2 eggs per person. Sprinkle some extra chives and dried chilli flakes over the top, and tuck in!

SERVES 4
30 mins

Bree Tranter
Tuesday Fresh Cuts

INGREDIENTS

300 g (1½ cups) brown rice
3 avocados
2 vine tomatoes
1 lime
3 spring onions (scallions)
fresh coriander (cilantro)
300 g (10½ oz) tofu

ZINGY VEGAN BLACK BEAN & AVOCADO BURRITOS [VG]

01   Boil the brown rice using the ratio: 1 part rice, 2 parts water, until the water has been absorbed.

02   Meanwhile, get on with your guac. Add the flesh of the avocados to a bowl. Finely chop the vine tomatoes and add to the bowl. Add the juice of a lime along with the chopped spring onions and a handful of chopped coriander. Season with salt and pepper and mash together. Cover and set aside.

03   Scrambled tofu time. Crumble the tofu into a bowl. Grate in the garlic, and add 2½ tablespoons of soy sauce. Add some black pepper.

1½ garlic cloves
soy sauce
1 x 400-g (14-oz) tin of black beans
8 tortllla wraps
salt and pepper

04 Get a pan on the heat. Add your tofu and cook for 4–5 minutes until it starts to catch on the pan. When it does, remove it from the heat.

05 When the rice is ready, drain, and then add the black beans. Lightly mash them together.

06 Lay out a couple of tortilla wraps. Fill them with equal parts of rice, tofu and guac. Roll them up, and then place, seam-side down, in a hot frying pan (skillet). Cook for 4–5 minutes on each side, or until golden and toasted. The mixture should make enough for 8 wraps.

07 Slice each wrap in half and get munching.

A GREAT DISH FOR A WEEKEND BRUNCH, OR FOR WEEKDAY MEAL PREP. SUPER HEALTHY AND SUPER VEGAN. ONE OF THE SQUIDGIEST MOUTHFULS YOU'LL EVER TAKE!

Fela Kuti
Zombie

INGREDIENTS

1 brown onion
2 garlic cloves
1 red chilli
2 (bell) peppers
1 x 250-g (9-oz) chorizo ring
2 x 400-g (14-oz) tins of
chopped tomatoes
eggs
200 g (7 oz) feta
fresh parsley

**THIS RECIPE WILL CHANGE
THE WAY YOU LOOK AT
BREAKFAST FOREVER. THE
BEAUTIFUL, RICH TOMATO
SAUCE AND THE CRISPY
CHORIZO MAKE IT A
STRAIGHT 10/10.**

01   Preheat the oven to 180°C fan (200°C/400°F/Gas Mark 6).

02   Finely chop the brown onion, garlic cloves and red chilli.
Cut the peppers into strips, and cut the chorizo ring in half
and then into slices.

03   Add the chorizo to a big ovenproof frying pan (skillet) and fry
until crisp. Then add the vegetables. Fry until slightly softened,
for 5–6 minutes, then add the chopped tomatoes. Fill up
both tomato tins with water, and pour that in as well. Give it
a stir and let it bubble away. You want the sauce to be a thick
consistency, so allow it reduce by around half.

04   Take the sauce off the heat and smooth out the surface.
Make little holes in the sauce and gently drop in 8 eggs, so
the yolks stay intact. Turn the heat back to medium, cover with
a lid and cook for 5 minutes. Then place the whole pan into
the hot oven for about 10 minutes until the eggs are cooked.

05   Remove the pan, and crumble in the feta. Add some chopped
parsley and get stuck in!

THE ULTIMATE PANCAKES (4 WAYS)

MAKES 8
30 mins

Boogie Belgique
Volta

THESE THIN PANCAKES ARE PERFECT FOR BREAKFAST, LUNCH OR DINNER. START A PRODUCTION LINE WITH YOUR FAVOURITE FILLING AND WRAP UP WITH YOUR MOB! MY FAVOURITE IS THE MUSHROOM ONE!

MUSHROOM, RICOTTA, THYME & LEMON ZEST PANCAKES

INGREDIENTS

500 g (1 lb 2 oz) chestnut mushrooms
1 garlic clove
fresh thyme
1 lemon
plain (all-purpose) flour
2 large (US extra-large) eggs
whole milk
ricotta
olive oil
salt and pepper

01 Finely slice the mushrooms and garlic. Chuck them in a frying pan (skillet) with a splash of olive oil. Cook the mushrooms down until the water has evaporated and they start to brown. This should take around 10 minutes. Be patient. They will look very watery as they start cooking, but this will evaporate.

02 Halfway through cooking the mushrooms, add a small handful of thyme leaves – about 3 teaspoons.

03 When the mushrooms are finished, grate in the zest of half a lemon and set aside.

04 Now for the batter. Place 100 g (1 scant cup) of flour, the eggs, 200 ml (1 cup minus 3 tablespoons) of milk and 100 ml (7 tablespoons) of cold water into a bowl. Beat it all together until there are no lumps of flour.

05 Heat a couple of teaspoons of olive oil in a non-stick frying pan over a medium–high heat. When it's really hot, ladle in some batter. It should cover the base of the pan thinly.

06 Give it 1–2 minutes on each side, but check with a spatula to see if the underside is cooked. Spoon on some mushrooms, a few dollops of ricotta, some more thyme leaves, a grate more lemon zest and some salt and pepper. And you're there!

PARMA HAM, GUACAMOLE & CHIVE PANCAKES

INGREDIENTS

3 large avocados
1 lemon
fresh chives
plain (all-purpose) flour
2 large (US extra-large) eggs
whole milk
1–2 x packs of Parma ham
salt and pepper
olive oil

01 First up, the guac. Halve the avocados and place the flesh in a bowl. Add almost all the juice of a lemon along with some salt, pepper and olive oil. Add a small handful of chopped chives and mash.

02 Now for the batter. Place 100 g (1 scant cup) of flour, the eggs, 200 ml (1 cup minus 3 tablespoons) of milk and 100 ml (7 tablespoons) of cold water into a bowl. Beat it all together until there are no lumps of flour. Add a small handful of chopped chives (leave a few to garnish).

03 Heat a couple of teaspoons of olive oil in a non-stick frying pan (skillet) over a medium–high heat. When it's really hot, ladle in the first helping of pancake mix. It should cover the base of the pan thinly.

04 Give it 1–2 minutes on each side, but just check with a spatula to see when the underside is cooked. Spoon on some guacamole and a slice of Parma ham. Sprinkle over a little more lemon juice and the last of the chopped chives. Done and dusted.

ASIAN SWEET POTATO PANCAKES

INGREDIENTS

3 sweet potatoes
fresh coriander (cilantro)
soy sauce
400 g (14 oz) spinach
plain (all-purpose) flour
2 large (US extra-large) eggs
whole milk
1 red chilli
5 spring onions (scallions)
fresh ginger
1 lemon
salt and pepper
olive oil

01 Preheat the oven to 180°C fan (200°C/400°F/Gas Mark 6). Place the sweet potatoes on a baking sheet. Cover in salt, pepper and olive oil. Bake for 50 minutes until soft.

02 Remove the sweet potato flesh, and place into a bowl. Take a small handful of coriander and finely chop it. Add it to the sweet potato and mash together, then add 3 tablespoons of soy sauce. Set aside.

03 Place the spinach into a frying pan (skillet) over a medium heat. Add some salt and pepper, and move it around with a wooden spoon until it has wilted (1–2 minutes). Set aside.

04 Follow step 4 of the recipe opposite to make the batter. Add 3 tablespoons of soy sauce, a finely chopped red chilli, 5 spring onions and grate in a thumb-sized piece of ginger.

05 Heat a couple of teaspoons of olive oil in a non-stick frying pan over a medium–high heat. When it's really hot, ladle in the first helping of pancake mix. It should cover the base of the pan thinly. Give it 1–2 minutes on each side, but just check with a spatula to see when the underside is cooked.

06 Once cooked, spoon on some of the sweet potato mash and some wilted spinach. Scatter more coriander and chopped spring onions over the top and pour on a few more drops of soy sauce. Sprinkle over a few drops of lemon juice. Roll it up, take a bite and taste the rainbow!

LEEK & SMOKED STREAKY BACON PANCAKES

INGREDIENTS

8 leeks
300 g (10½ oz) smoked streaky bacon
plain (all-purpose) flour
2 large (US extra-large) eggs
whole milk
olive oil

01 Finely slice 8 leeks. Place into a large frying pan (skillet) with a good glug of olive oil. Cook over a medium–low heat until soft. Add small splashes of water if it looks like the leeks are catching on the bottom of the pan. They should be smooth and soft after about 12–15 minutes. Set aside.

02 In the meantime, fry the smoked streaky bacon. Once it is crisp, allow it to cool and then chop into bite-sized chunks.

03 Now for the batter. Place 100 g (1 scant cup) of flour, the eggs, 200 ml (1 cup minus 3 tablespoons) of milk and 100 ml (7 tablespoons) of cold water into a bowl. Beat it all together until there are no lumps of flour.

04 Heat a couple of teaspoons of olive oil in a non-stick frying pan over a medium–high heat. When it's really hot, ladle in the first helping of pancake mix. It should cover the base of the pan thinly.

05 Give it 1–2 minutes on each side, but just check with a spatula to see when the underside is cooked. Once cooked, spoon on some of your leeks, as well as a small handful of the crispy bacon. Then serve. Easy as 1, 2, 3!

CAPONATA FRITTATA [V]

SERVES 4
30 mins

The Bamboos
The Wilhelm Scream

INGREDIENTS

1 red onion
2 aubergines (eggplants)
100 g (¾ cup) pine nuts
250 g (9 oz) cherry tomatoes
fresh parsley
pitted green olives
capers
red wine vinegar
8 eggs
salt and pepper

SUCH A FRESH BREAKFAST OPTION. THE ZINGINESS OF THE CAPONATA REALLLLLY WORKS. IT'S ALSO RIDICULOUSLY DELICIOUS WHEN EATEN COLD.

01 Preheat the oven to 180°C fan (200°C/400°F/Gas Mark 6).

02 Finely chop the red onion and chop the aubergines into small cubes.

03 Add your aubergines to a wide, ovenproof frying pan (skillet) and brown off the cubes.

04 Meanwhile, toast the pine nuts in a separate pan.

05 Once the aubergine is browned, add your onion and the cherry tomatoes. Throw in a large handful of chopped parsley stalks (keep the leaves separate).

06 When the tomatoes and onion are softened, add 2 tablespoons of sliced green olives and 1 tablespoon of capers. Pour in 3 tablespoons of red wine vinegar and cook over a high heat until the vinegar has evaporated.

07 Add the toasted pine nuts and a large handful of chopped parsley leaves (keep a few to serve) and mix them through the caponata.

08 In a bowl, whisk up the eggs. Season with pepper.

09 Pour the eggs into the caponata. Mix them around so everything is evenly spread.

10 Cook the frittata over a medium heat for 5 minutes, and then place in the hot oven for a further 5 minutes until the eggs have set.

11 Serve the dish with the leftover parsley leaves, season to your taste and munch away! It will be the best breakfast mouthful you'll ever have.

LEBANESE HALLOUMI EGGS [V]

SERVES 4
20 mins

Palace
Veins

INGREDIENTS

1 x 150-g (5½-oz) pot of
hummus
1 lemon
400 g (14 oz) halloumi
1 garlic clove
1 red chilli
200 g (7 oz) curly kale
fresh ginger
8 eggs
1 large ciabatta loaf
salt and pepper
olive oil

**THE MAGIC OF THIS
DISH IS IN THE COMBO.
A FORKFUL OF THIS,
A FORKFUL OF THAT.
DIPPING, SCOOPING,
MIXING, SHARING...
IT'S A BEAUTYYY!**

01 Hummus dressing time. Add the hummus to a bowl, squeeze in the juice of a lemon and season with salt and pepper. Add a small glug of olive oil and stir it together.

02 Slice the halloumi into generous slabs.

03 Finely chop the garlic and chilli. Peel a small piece of ginger and slice it up into matchsticks.

04 Get a pan on the heat and splash in some olive oil. Throw in your garlic, chilli and ginger, and fry for 1 minute. Then add your kale with a small splash of water. Fry it until it is soft, but still with a crunchy centre. Set the pan aside.

05 Beat the eggs in a bowl. Season with salt and pepper. Add a splash of olive oil. Pour them into a non-stick frying pan (skillet). As the bottom layer starts cooking, move lines through it with a wooden spoon. Keep folding the eggs like this until they are all cooked.

06 In the meantime, get your halloumi slabs onto a hot griddle pan. Cook for 3–4 minutes on each side.

07 Toast 8 slices of ciabatta.

08 To serve up, place 2 ciabatta slices on each plate. Drizzle some olive oil over it, and then spoon over the eggs. Add a generous spoonful of the kale, pour over some hummus dressing and finish the plate with a couple of nice slabs of grilled halloumi. Load up your fork with all the elements and tuck in.

INGREDIENTS

4 red (bell) peppers

1 x 250-g (9-oz) chorizo ring

mayonnaise

4 small ciabatta rolls

fresh basil

manchego cheese
(about 200 g/7 oz)

salted butter

olive oil

salt and pepper

THIS TAKES A LITTLE BIT OF EFFORT, BUT I PROMISE YOU THAT ONCE YOU GET THERE IT IS SO SO WORTH IT. SO MUCH BETTER THAN THE EGG AND BACON NORM... AN ABSOLUTE WORLDY OF A SANDY!

THE ULTIMATE HUNGOVER SANDWICH

01 Preheat the oven to 180°C fan (200°C/400°F/Gas Mark 6).

02 Chop the peppers into big chunks and add to a roasting pan, drizzle with olive oil, season with salt and pepper and roast for 45 minutes or until charred and soft.

03 Meanwhile, crumble the chorizo into a frying pan (skillet). Cook over a medium heat until the chorizo is crispy and the oil has rendered out. Add the chorizo and 2 tablespoons of chorizo oil to a bowl. Add 5 tablespoons of mayonnaise and mix it all together.

04 Loading time. Warm the ciabatta rolls in the oven. Halve them. Lather on some chorizo mayo. Then add a layer of peppers. Then add a couple of basil leaves, followed by some manchego slices. Spread some salted butter on the top half of the ciabatta, place it on the top and take the biggest bite your mouth can manage.

SQUIDGY CARBONARA CRUMPETS

SERVES 4
20 mins

 ᐧᐧᐧᐧᐧᐧᐧᐧᐧᐧᐧᐧᐧᐧᐧᐧ

Andras Fox
Your Life

INGREDIENTS

1 x 200-g (7-oz) pack of smoked
bacon lardons
6 eggs
Parmesan cheese
8 crumpets
salt and pepper

**SOUNDS WEIRD BUT
THIS RECIPE IS THE ONE.
SQUIDGY CRUMPETS,
SMOKEY, CRISPY BACON,
SALTY PARMESAN. IDEAL
FOR THE HUNGOVER MOB.
SO CHEAP YOU COULD
ALMOST MAKE THIS
ONE TWICE**

01 Add the lardons to a frying pan (skillet) and cook them over a medium heat until very crispy.

02 In the meantime, whisk up the eggs in a bowl using a fork. Add 70 g (1 cup) of grated Parmesan and season generously with black pepper. It should be very peppery so go wild with the grinding. Whisk everything together, and set aside.

03 Once the bacon is crispy, remove it from the heat. KEEP THE PAN WITH THE BACON FAT!

04 Pour the bacon bits into the egg mixture and mix it in.

05 Dunking time. Dunk each crumpet into the egg mixture for at least 30 seconds so it can absorb the eggy mixture.

06 Place your crumpets, hole-side down, in the bacon fat pan, pouring over any excess bacony bits. Give it a good press with a spatula.

07 Fry for 3–4 minutes on each side over a medium heat until golden, and then remove from the heat. Serve with an extra grating of Parmesan and enjoy!

INGREDIENTS

1 kg (2 lbs 3 oz) frozen peas
70 g (½ cup) pine nuts
1 large garlic clove
Parmesan cheese
fresh basil
fresh mint
1 lemon
200 g (7 oz) spinach
8 eggs
olive oil
salt and pepper

ONE FOR ALL THE GREEN FIENDS. THE FRESHEST BAKED EGGS IN TOWN. DR. SEUSS WOULD BE PROUD.

GREEN BAKED EGGS [V]

01   Preheat the oven to 180°C fan (200°C/400°F/Gas Mark 6).

02   Pour the frozen peas into a saucepan and cover them with boiling water. Bubble away over a high heat until cooked.

03   Toast the pine nuts in a dry frying pan (skillet) over a medium heat, stirring often until golden. Don't let them burn. Set aside.

04   Remove the peas from the heat. Drain them, and pour half of them into a blender. Add the garlic, 80 g (1¼ cups) of grated Parmesan, two-thirds of the toasted pine nuts, a handful of chopped basil, a handful of chopped mint, and salt and pepper. Add a glug of olive oil and a small splash of water. Blitz until smooth. Squeeze in the juice of a lemon and blitz again.

05   Gently mash the other peas and set aside.

06   Wilt the spinach in a large, ovenproof pan. Once wilted, add your mashed-up peas, leftover toasted pine nuts and the pea purée. Mix everything together. Make 8 wells in the base of the pan and crack in your eggs.

07   Place the dish in the hot oven for 11 minutes or until the eggs are set. Scatter over any leftover herbs, a heaped tablespoon of grated Parmesan and tuck in!

INGREDIENTS

1 x 200-g (7-oz) pack of smoked
bacon lardons
1 brown onion
1 red (bell) pepper
2 garlic cloves
1 red chilli
herbes de Provence
ground cumin
brown sugar
1–2 bottles of beer (we used
Corona)
2 x 400-g (14-oz) tins of red
kidney beans
fresh coriander (cilantro)
1 white sourdough loaf
salt and pepper

BAD BOY BACON BAKED BEANS ON TOAST

01 Add the lardons to a large frying pan (skillet) and cook over a medium heat until crispy.

02 Finely chop the brown onion and chop the pepper into small cubes. Slice up the garlic and chilli.

03 Add the veg to the frying pan, with 1 heaped teaspoon of herbes de Provence and ½ teaspoon of cumin. Mix it together, and fry down until the onions and peppers are soft. Add 1 heaped teaspoon of sugar and mix it in.

04 At this point, pour in 400 ml (14 fl oz) of beer. Cook over a high heat for 30 seconds, and then add the kidney beans (rinsed and drained).

05 Turn the heat down to medium and continue cooking without a lid for 15 minutes until most of the beer has evaporated and the beans are soft. Season with salt and pepper, throw in a large handful of chopped coriander and serve on hot, crunchy sourdough toast.

CHANGING THE BAKED-BEAN GAME FOREVER. PERFECT IF YOU'VE GOT A LEFTOVER LAGER IN THE FRIDGE THAT NEEDS FINISHING OFF. GO HEAVY WITH THE CORIANDER AT THE END – IT REALLY BRINGS THE KICK.

FRESH MOB

INGREDIENTS

1 large butternut squash
1 red onion
½ garlic clove
tahini
1 lemon
100 g (¾ cup) pine nuts
200 g (7 oz) kale
225 g (8 oz) halloumi cheese
1 x pack of pomegranate seeds
fresh mint
olive oil
salt and pepper

**THE MOST SCRUMPTIOUS
SALAD YOU'LL EVER
MUNCH AT HOME. THE
TAHINI DRESSING IS
EVERYTHING. MAKE SURE
YOU GET THOSE PINE
NUTS NICE AND TOASTY.**

THE ULTIMATE HALLOUMI, BUTTERNUT SQUASH & TAHINI SALAD [V] [★]

01 Preheat the oven to 180°C fan (200°C/400°F/Gas Mark 6).

02 Cut up the butternut squash into cubes and chop the red onion into chunks. Add to a roasting pan. Drizzle with olive oil and season with salt and pepper. Place in the hot oven for 30 minutes or until the veg is caramelized and soft.

03 Dressing time. Grate the garlic and add to a bowl along with 3 tablespoons of tahini, the juice of a lemon, a big pinch of salt and pepper and a tablespoon of olive oil. Mix everything together. Add warm water until you have a thick, creamy consistency. Set the dressing aside.

04 Toast the pine nuts in a dry frying pan (skillet). Set aside.

05 Steam the kale until cooked through (7–8 minutes). Set aside.

06 Cut the halloumi into thick slices.

07 When the onions and the butternut squash are ready, remove them from the oven.

08 Get a griddle pan on the heat (use a frying pan if you don't have a griddle), add a drizzle of olive oil, and then add the halloumi slices.

09 Cook over a high heat for 3 minutes on each side.

10 Assembly time. Add the butternut squash, onion, kale, most of the toasted pine nuts, 60 g (2 oz) of pomegranate seeds, and a good handful of chopped mint. Mix everything together. Pour the tahini dressing over the top, and mix it in.

11 Top the salad with the remaining pine nuts, a few more pomegranate seeds and some mint leaves. Spoon it out and get stuck in!

William DeVaughn
Be Thankful for What
You Got

INGREDIENTS

4 sweet potatoes
dried chilli flakes
1 brown onion
2 (bell) peppers (not green)
1 red chilli
spring onions (scallions)
2 garlic cloves
ground cumin
paprika
1 x 400-g (14-oz) tin of black
beans
Cheddar cheese
1–2 limes
olive oil
salt and pepper

FOR THE GUAC

2 large avocados
fresh coriander (cilantro)
1 lime
1 red chilli

HOLY MOLY, THIS ONE'S A
HIT THAT TICKS ALL THE
BOXES. THE GUAC IS OUT
OF THIS WORLD. SUCH A
SATISFYING VEGGIE DISH.

MEXICAN-STYLE STUFFED SWEET POTATOES [V] [★]

01　Preheat the oven to 180°C fan (200°C/400°F/Gas Mark 6).

02　Drizzle the sweet potatoes in olive oil, and sprinkle over salt and a small handful of dried chilli flakes. Bake them in the hot oven for 50 minutes or until soft.

03　While the sweet potatoes are in the oven, sort the guac. Scoop the flesh out of the avocados and add to a bowl. Add a handful of chopped coriander (save some to garnish), the juice of a lime, a finely chopped red chilli, some salt, pepper and olive oil. Mish mash.

04　Finely chop the brown onion, peppers, chilli and a bunch of spring onions.

05　In a pan, add a splash of olive oil. Add chopped garlic, 2 teaspoons of ground cumin and 2 teaspoons of paprika. Once the garlic has softened (1 minute), add the peppers and brown onion. Fry until soft, on a medium–low heat. This should take about 10–15 minutes. Add a bit of water if it starts catching on the pan.

06　Once softened, chuck in the black beans. Mash everything together well.

07　Remove your sweet potatoes from the oven. Scoop out the flesh, and save the skins. Add the flesh to the black bean chilli. Mix everything together.

08　Assembly time. Re-stuff the sweet potato skins with the black bean chilli. Add a big dollop of guac. Top with a generous grating of Cheddar, and garnish with the chopped spring onions, chopped red chilli and remaining coriander. Squeeze over some lime juice to finish. Enjoy!

INGREDIENTS

chicken stock (bouillon) cubes
star anise
coriander seeds
fish sauce
lemongrass purée
fresh ginger
1 x 500-g (1-lb 2 oz) pack of
diced chicken breasts
300 g (10½ oz) rice noodles
fresh coriander (cilantro)
1 red chilli

**THE MOST WARMING,
FLAVOURFUL BROTH. AND
IF YOU'VE GOT A COLD,
THIS RECIPE WILL KNOCK
IT OUT OF THE PARK.**

CHICKEN PHO-MO

01 Add 1 litre (quart) of water to a large pot. Add 2 good-quality chicken stock cubes and mix them in. Then add 2 star anise and 1 tablespoon of coriander seeds. Add 1 tablespoon of fish sauce, 2 teaspoons of lemongrass purée and a peeled and grated 5-cm (2-inch) piece of ginger. Then plop in the diced chicken breasts.

02 Cook over a medium heat for 10 minutes until the chicken is cooked through. Remove the chicken and shred it on a board. Then add the rice noodles to the soup. These should take 2–3 minutes to cook through.

03 Once ready, add some rice noodles and the shredded chicken to 4 bowls. Add a handful of coriander, a few slices of red chilli and then pour over your soup.

04 Get a spoon and tuck in!

INGREDIENTS

3 minute steaks
2 red (bell) peppers
2 Cos (romaine) lettuces
1 cucumber
1 watermelon
fresh ginger
1 red chilli
fresh mint
2 limes
sesame oil
fish sauce
olive oil
salt and pepper

SO EASY TO THROW TOGETHER, AND USING MINUTE STEAKS MAKES IT AFFORDABLE. THE MAGIC LIES IN THE DRESSING, FOLLOW IT TO THE LETTER.

THAI MINUTE STEAK SALAD

01 Let the minute steaks get to room temperature. Lay them on a board and place a layer of clingfilm (plastic wrap) over them. Give them a light bash with a rolling pin, and then place them on a plate. Season with salt, pepper and olive oil, and let them sit for 10 minutes.

02 The rest of this is really just an assembly job. Cut the peppers into long strips and add them to a large salad bowl. Chop the lettuces finely and add. Peel and halve a cucumber. Chop the halves in half, and scoop out the watery seeds. Then slice the cucumber into matchsticks, and add to the bowl. Cut your watermelon into big, bite-sized chunks (you'll need about 90 g/3 oz) and add to the bowl.

03 Grate in a peeled small piece of ginger and a red chilli. Finely chop a large handful of mint and add that.

04 Dressing time. This part is important. Add the juice of 2 limes, 1½ teaspoons of sesame oil, 2 tablespoons of fish sauce and 2 tablespoons of olive oil to a bowl. Mix everything together.

05 Steak time. Get a griddle pan on the heat. Once it is nice and hot, add the steaks, one by one. Cook for 1 minute on each side so it's still nice and pink in the middle.

06 Let the steaks rest on a plate for 5 minutes, and then slice them very thinly. Add to the salad bowl, and then pour over your dressing. Toss everything together and serve up!

INGREDIENTS

1 whole chicken
sesame seeds
6 courgettes (zucchini)
1 cucumber
1 large lettuce – your choice!
fresh coriander (cilantro)
1 red chilli
fresh ginger
1 lime
soy sauce
olive oil
salt and pepper

SUCH A MOREISH MEAL – YOU WON'T BE ABLE TO STOP EATING. AND... THE DRESSING PRETTY MUCH WORKS WITH ANYTHING – FISH, VEG, MEAT – SO IT'S A GREAT ONE TO LEARN.

ASIAN COURGETTE RIBBON & CHICKEN SALAD [★]

01   Preheat the oven to 170°C fan (190°C/375°F/Gas Mark 5).

02   Place the chicken in a roasting pan. Season with salt and pepper, and drizzle with olive oil. Place in the hot oven to cook for 1 hour and 20 minutes.

03   Toast a large handful of sesame seeds in a dry frying pan (skillet). Set aside.

04   Get a peeler. Halve the courgettes and peel off the skin, and then peel them into ribbons.

05   Halve the cucumber and peel off the skin, and then peel into ribbons. When you get to the watery core, turn it and peel the other side. You don't want the watery bit. Place the ribbons in the salad bowl.

06   Remove the chicken from the oven. Carve it, shred the meat and throw it into the salad bowl.

07   Add a chopped lettuce, the toasted sesame seeds (leave a few to garnish), a handful of chopped coriander (leave some to garnish) and a sliced chilli to the salad bow!. Grate in a 5-cm (2-inch) piece of peeled ginger. Squeeze in the juice of a lime and pour in 4–5 tablespoons of soy sauce and 3 tablespoons of olive oil.

08   Mix everything together. Scatter the leftover sesame seeds and coriander leaves on top and serve!

INGREDIENTS

2 sweet potatoes
250 g (1½ cups) quinoa
2 avocados
2 Granny Smith apples
celery
2 lemons
Dijon mustard
olive oil
200 g (7 oz) feta cheese

THE DREAM MEAL-PREP
SALAD, SO EASY, SO TASTY.
THE COMBO OF THE
APPLE AND THE CELERY IS
EVERYTHING – MAKE SURE
YOU USE BOTH!

SWEET POTATO, FETA & AVOCADO QUINOA SALAD [V]

01 Preheat the oven to 180°C fan (200°C/400°F/Gas Mark 6).

02 Peel the sweet potatoes and cut up them into cubes. Place on a baking sheet in the hot oven for 40 minutes or until soft.

03 Quinoa time. This part is important. Rinse the quinoa thoroughly. Then add it to a pan with 3 parts boiling water. Bring to the boil, then turn down to a simmer and cover for 15 minutes until the water has been absorbed. Turn the heat off and leave the quinoa in the pan for 3 more minutes, with the lid on, which will allow it to steam. Place the quinoa in a sieve (strainer) and run cold water through it. Drain thoroughly, and then add to a large salad bowl.

04 De-stone the avocados and cut into cubes. Peel the apples, core them and chop into bite-sized cubes. Slice 3 stalks (ribs) of celery into bite-sized chunks. Add everything to the quinoa in the salad bowl.

05 Dressing time. Add the juice of the lemons, 2 teaspoons of Dijon mustard and 5 tablespoons of olive oil to a jar, and mix together.

06 Remove the sweet potato from the oven and chuck it into the bowl.

07 Crumble the feta into the salad bowl.

08 Pour the dressing over the salad and toss everything together. Serve up and enjoy!

INGREDIENTS

400 g (14 oz) firm tofu (we used
The Tofoo Co.)
fresh ginger
soy sauce
1 red chilli
1 x 400-ml (14-fl oz) tin of
coconut milk
smooth peanut butter
1 lime
400 g (2¼ cups) brown rice
1 head of broccoli
2 carrots
sesame oil
peanuts
fresh coriander (cilantro)

**A VEGAN DREAM OF A
BOWL. THE CRUNCHY
PEANUTS, THE GRILLED
TOFU, THE CREAMY
PEANUT SAUCE. WHAT
MORE COULD YOU WANT?**

GRIDDLED TOFU BUDDHA BOWL WITH PEANUT SAUCE [VG]

01 Cut the tofu into strips and place in a bowl. Grate a 5-cm (2-inch) piece of peeled ginger and add almost all of it to the bowl along with 2 tablespoons of soy sauce and a grated red chilli. Add half a tin of coconut milk and mix everything together well.

02 Time for the peanut butter sauce. Into a bowl, add 1 heaped tablespoon of peanut butter, the remaining grated ginger, the other half of the tin of coconut milk, the juice of ½ lime and 1 tablespoon of soy sauce. Mix everything together. If it is too loose, add a bit more peanut butter until you have a thick sauce. Set aside.

03 Get the brown rice on – add 1 part rice to 2 parts water and boil until the water has been absorbed.

04 Cut a head of broccoli into florets and steam it.

05 Peel the carrots into ribbons.

06 To cook the tofu, add it to a griddle or frying pan (skillet) and cook each strip for 2 minutes on each side, over a medium–high heat.

07 When the broccoli is cooked, and still a bit crunchy, remove from the heat. Toss it in 1 teaspoon of sesame oil.

08 Plate up. Add a layer of rice to a bowl. Then add some tofu on one side, some sesame broccoli on another side and some carrot in the leftover space. Pour your peanut butter sauce over the tofu. Sprinkle over a handful of chopped peanuts and throw on a handful of coriander. Enjoy!

INGREDIENTS

1 onion

2 garlic cloves

fresh parsley

cumin seeds

500 g (1 lb 2 oz) lamb mince

1 x 500-g (18-oz) pot of Greek yogurt

1 cucumber

fresh mint

1 lemon

400 g (2½ cups) couscous

watercress

1 x pack of pomegranate seeds

olive oil

salt and pepper

THESE DELICIOUS, SUPER-SIMPLE HERBY KOFTAS WITH TZATZIKI MAKE THE PERFECT LUNCH OR SPEEDY DINNER.

LAMB KOFTA COUSCOUS SALAD WITH TZATZIKI

01   Chop the onion and garlic. Whack them into a frying pan (skillet) with a dash of olive oil over a medium heat. Add 2 tablespoons of chopped parsley stalks and 1 tablespoon of cumin seeds. Once the onions are soft, take them off the heat and allow to cool.

02   Put the lamb mince into a mixing bowl and add the cooked onion mixture, as well as a splash of olive oil, some salt and a pinch of pepper. Mix it all up.

03   Roll the lamb mixture into little golf balls and flatten them into kofta shapes, so they are around 1 cm (½ inch) thick.

04   Place on a plate, cover with clingfilm (plastic wrap) and put them in the fridge to firm up (10–15 minutes will do).

05   Now for the tzatziki. Add the yogurt, a grated cucumber (squeeze out the grated cucumber to remove any excess liquid), a chopped bunch of mint (save a few leaves to garnish) and juice of a lemon to a mixing bowl and add a sprinkling of salt. Mix well.

06   Back to your koftas. Take them out of the fridge and heat a griddle pan. Drizzle a little oil on each kofta and place them in the pan over a medium–high heat. Griddle the koftas for 5–6 minutes, turning halfway through so that both sides are well browned.

07   Cook the couscous according to the packet instructions. Fluff it up with a fork.

08   Once the koftas are cooked, throw over a handful of chopped parsley and allow it to stick to the outside of the koftas.

09   Serving time. Mix a small handful of watercress through the couscous. Serve the koftas on top of the couscous salad with a small handful of pomegranate seeds and your remaining mint scattered on top. Dollop your tzatziki over everything and dive in!

INGREDIENTS

1 lime
4 salmon fillets
fresh ginger
1–2 red chillies
fresh coriander (cilantro)
soy sauce
400 g (2¼ cups) wild rice

A QUICK, LIGHT, HEALTHY
DINNER. NO ADDED FAT.
PERFECT FOR POST-GYM
OR PRE-NIGHT OUT. SO
EASY TO DO, AND THE
STEAMING MEANS IT
DOESN'T LEAVE YOUR
CLOTHES SMELLING LIKE
FRIED FISH. IDEAL.

GINGER STEAMED SALMON WITH WILD RICE

01 Preheat the oven to 180°C fan (200°C/400°F/Gas Mark 6).

02 Cut the lime into thin slices and place them on a baking sheet. Lay the salmon fillets on top of the slices.

03 Add a peeled, chopped, thumb-sized piece of ginger, a chopped chilli and a handful of chopped coriander stalks to the sheet. Add a small glass of water, and the same amount of soy sauce.

04 Cover the sheet TIGHTLY in foil (you don't want any of the steam to escape).

05 Bake in the hot oven for 12 minutes.

06 While the salmon is in the oven, put the wild rice (in the ratio 1 part rice to 2 parts boiling water) into a pan and boil until the water has been absorbed.

07 Take the salmon out of the oven. Remove the foil, and scatter over some coriander leaves and an extra sliced red chilli, if you want an extra kick of heat.

08 Serve the salmon on top of the rice with all the juices poured on top.

CHICKEN PANZANELLA

INGREDIENTS

1 large ciabatta loaf
300 g (10½ oz) chicken breasts
6–8 vine tomatoes
200 g (7 oz) cherry tomatoes
capers
4 shallots
150 g (5½ oz) roasted (bell)
peppers
250 g (9 oz) feta cheese
red wine vinegar
fresh basil
olive oil
salt and pepper

**THE FETA WORKS A TREAT
IN THIS CLASSIC AS IT
BRINGS A NICE SHARP HIT.
IDEAL FOR A SUMMER'S
EVENING WITH A COUPLE
OF GLASSES OF VINO.**

01 Preheat the oven to 180°C fan (200°C/400°F/Gas Mark 6).

02 Break the ciabatta loaf into bite-sized chunks. Add them to a baking sheet with a drizzle of olive oil and sprinkling of salt and pepper and toast them in the oven for around 10 minutes. Leave on a plate and set aside.

03 Chop up the chicken breasts into bite-sized pieces. Add the pieces to a griddle pan with a splash of olive oil over a medium heat. Griddle for 4–5 minutes until cooked through. Season with salt and pepper, then add to a large salad bowl.

04 Roughly chop the vine tomatoes, and cut the cherry tomatoes into quarters. Add them to the salad bowl. Add 1 tablespoon of capers, finely chopped shallots and sliced roasted peppers. Crumble in the feta. Then add your ciabatta chunks, and pour in 3 tablespoons of vinegar and 5 tablespoons of olive oil.

05 Season with salt and pepper, and add a large handful of basil. Toss it all together, making sure you squidge the bread in to soak up all of the juices.

06 Drizzle over some more olive oil and tuck in.

SPEEDY MOB

Y. Gershovsky
Disco Baby

INGREDIENTS

fresh mint
fresh coriander (cilantro)
fresh ginger
1 red chilli
4 spring onions (scallions)
300 g (10½ oz) basmati rice
500 g (1 lb 2 oz) pork mince
lemongrass purée
fish sauce
2–3 limes
1–2 crispy lettuces (depending
on size)
olive oil

**HEALTHY. FUN. FRESH. ALL
SERVED INSIDE A LETTUCE
LEAF. AMAZING FOR A
DINNER PARTY – HARDLY
ANY WASHING UP! WHAT
MORE COULD YOU WANT?**

THE FRESHEST THAI PORK LARB [★]

01 Prep your ingredients. Take a bunch of mint and one of coriander. With a knife, separate the stalks and the leaves. Finely chop both, but keep them separate. Peel a 5-cm (2-inch) piece of ginger and chop it into small matchsticks. Finely slice the chilli and spring onions.

02 At this point, get the basmati rice on. Rinse the rice, and then add it to a pan with double the amount of boiling water. Cook the rice without a lid until the water has been absorbed.

03 In a large wok or frying pan (skillet), add a splash of olive oil and then add your pork mince. Fry on a high heat, breaking it up with a wooden spoon. As the pork starts to caramelize, remove it from the wok and set it aside.

04 In the same wok, add a splash more oil, and then add your chopped ginger, sliced red chilli, mint and coriander stalks, spring onions and 2 teaspoons of lemongrass purée.

05 Keep mixing your larb base. Once it starts to catch on the pan, pour in 4 tablespoons of fish sauce and squeeze in the juice of a lime. Mix it together, and then reintroduce the pork mince. Stir and then add your rice spoon by spoon. Once all the rice and pork is folded together, add your coriander and mint leaves. Mix together, and then remove the larb from the heat.

06 Serve the larb in crispy lettuce leaves and cut up some lime wedges for squeezing. Enjoy!

INGREDIENTS

8 boneless, skinless chicken thighs
3 garlic cloves
1 red chilli
dried oregano
1 lemon
1 x 500-g (18-oz) pot of natural yogurt
fresh mint
1 cucumber
4–6 vine tomatoes
1 iceberg lettuce
4 large pittas
salt and pepper
olive oil

HEALTHY CHICKEN GYROS [★]

01 Dice the chicken thighs into small chunks. Add to a large bowl. Grate the garlic and chilli into the bowl. Add 3 teaspoons of oregano, the zest of a lemon, 3 tablespoons of yogurt and salt and pepper. Rub together and cover with clingfilm (plastic wrap). Put in the fridge to marinade for 15 minutes.

02 Tzatziki time. Pour the rest of the yogurt into another bowl. Chuck in a finely chopped small bunch of mint, the juice of the lemon and a grated cucumber (squeeze out the grated cucumber to remove any excess liquid). Season well and mix it all together.

03 Tomato salsa time. Deseed and finely chop the tomatoes. Add to a bowl with 2–3 teaspoons of dried oregano, salt, pepper and olive oil.

04 Finely chop the lettuce.

05 Put a griddle pan over a medium–high heat. Once it is hot, add your chicken chunks. They'll need 3 minutes on each side.

06 Warm the pittas in a toaster or in the microwave.

07 Assemble the gyros by adding the chicken, lettuce, salsa and tzatziki to the pittas and rolling them up. Tuck in!

SPICY CHICKEN IN WARM PITTAS, WITH A FRESH TOMATO SALSA AND THE PERFECT COOLING TZATZIKI. IT COULDN'T BE EASIER TO MAKE THIS GREEK CLASSIC. AND IT'S ALL FOR UNDER A TENNER. EASYYYY!

INGREDIENTS

1 x 250-g (9-oz) chorizo ring
dried chilli flakes
165 g (6 oz) raw king prawns
(jumbo shrimp)
1 garlic clove
500 g (1 lb 2 oz) passata
(strained tomatoes)
500 g (1 lb 2 oz) dried linguine
fresh basil
olive oil
salt and pepper

**THE NAUGHTIEST SURF 'N'
TURF COMBO ABOUT. SALTY,
CRISPY CHORIZO WITH
PLUMP, FRESH PRAWNS.**

PRAWN, CHORIZO & BASIL LINGUINE

01 Slice the chorizo into bite-sized pieces. Add to a frying pan (skillet) over a medium heat and cook until crispy.

02 Once crispy, add a pinch of dried chilli flakes and the raw prawns. Cook the prawns until they are pink, then add a chopped garlic clove. Cook for a further 30 seconds, and then pour in the passata.

03 Get the linguine on (follow the instructions on the packet).

04 Meanwhile, bubble the sauce down until it is nice and thick. Then throw in a handful of chopped basil (keep some whole leaves to garnish) and season well with salt and pepper.

05 Drain your pasta and pour it into the sauce. Mix everything together and serve, with a drizzle of olive oil and the basil leaves scattered on top.

SERVES 4
10 mins

Lack of Afro
The Basis

THE DIPPING SAUCE

crunchy peanut butter
soy sauce
fish sauce
honey
1 lime

SUPER QUICK VIETNAMESE SPRING ROLLS WITH A PEANUT DIPPING SAUCE

01 First the dipping sauce. Slowly add 2 heaped tablespoons of crunchy peanut butter to about 1 tablespoon of soy sauce, 4 teaspoons of fish sauce, 3 teaspoons of honey and 1 tablespoon of water until you have a paste. Then slowly add the juice of a lime and incorporate it. Adjust the sauce to taste with soy or honey. It should be quite loose, so add a splash more water if needed.

02 Cook the noodles (following the instructions on the packet).

400 g (14 oz) rice noodles
3 carrots
1 cucumber
2 red (bell) peppers
fresh coriander (cilantro)
fresh mint
sesame oil
8 spring roll wrappers

03 Prep your veg. Peel the carrots and the cucumber and chop into matchsticks. Deseed the peppers and chop into matchsticks. Add the veg to a big bowl. Add a large handful of chopped coriander, a large handful of chopped mint and 2 teaspoons of sesame oil. Mix everything together.

04 Place your spring roll wrappers on a plate. Submerge them one by one in boiling water for a few seconds and remove them carefully.

05 Once soft, take one wrapper in your hand. Fill it with some of your sesame veg, and then with some noodles. Wrap it up, and then dunk it in your dipping sauce and tuck in!

SO QUICK. SO EASY. SO FRESH. DUNK ONE
OF THESE CHEEKY LITTLE MONKEYS IN THAT
PEANUT SAUCE AND GET TRANSPORTED TO
TASTE HEAVEN.

INGREDIENTS

2 corn on the cobs
3 (bell) peppers (red, orange
or yellow)
1 cucumber
1 red onion
160 g (5½ oz) smoked tofu
1 x 400-g (14-oz) tin of black
beans
1 red chilli
3 spring onions (scallions)
fresh coriander (cilantro)
2 limes
olive oil

**A GREAT SALLY SHOUT
FOR YOUR SUMMER. THE
FIRM, SMOKEY TOFU
WORKS A CHARM WITH
THE ZINGY DRESSING.**

VEGAN CARIBBEAN SALAD [VG]

01 Preheat the oven to 180°C fan (200°C/400°F/Gas Mark 6).

02 Take the corn on the cobs. Wrap each one tightly in foil, place on a baking sheet, and place in the hot oven for 30 minutes.

03 Meanwhile, finely chop the peppers, cucumber and red onion into little chunks. Whack it all in a big salad bowl.

04 Take the smoked tofu and chop it into bite-sized cubes. Add to the salad bowl.

05 Remove the corn on the cobs from the oven, cut off the corn kernels, and place them in the salad bowl along with the black beans.

06 Slice up the chilli and add it to the salad bowl along with the chopped spring onions and a large handful of chopped coriander (leaving some leaves for the garnish). Add the juice of 2 limes and a drizzle of olive oil. Mix everything together.

07 Scatter the leftover coriander and serve!

INGREDIENTS

50 g (scant ½ cup) pine nuts
fresh mint
fresh basil
Parmesan cheese
1 lemon
2 garlic cloves
500 g (1 lb 2 oz) gnocchi
chives
olive oil

QUICK HOMEMADE PESTO. COMFORTING GNOCCHI. SUCH A CHEAP MID-WEEK DINNER. MAKE SURE YOU KEEP AN EYE ON THE PINE NUTS AS THEY ARE TOASTING, THOUGH – THEY CAN BURN VERY QUICKLY!

SPEEDY PESTO GNOCCHI [V]

01 Toast your pine nuts in a dry frying pan (skillet) for a few minutes. Make sure they don't burn – keep watching them!

02 Add a large handful of mint, a large handful of basil, almost all of the toasted pine nuts, 80 g (1¼ cups) of grated Parmesan, the zest and juice of a lemon and the garlic into a blender. Add 5 tablespoons of olive oil and blitz until smooth.

03 Get the gnocchi on (follow the instructions on the packet).

04 Once the gnocchi is cooked, drain it. Toss your pesto in with the gnocchi. Throw in a handful of chopped chives and mix them in. Serve with leftover pine nuts and herbs scattered on top.

05 Dig your fork in and enjoy.

10-MINUTE PEANUT BUTTER DAN DAN NOODLES [V]

SERVES 4
10 mins

As Mamas
The Lights Are On But
Everyone's Wasted

INGREDIENTS

smooth peanut butter
soy sauce
2 garlic cloves
2–3 spring onions (scallions)
agave nectar
rice wine vinegar
Szechuan peppercorns
fresh ginger
vegetable oil
320 g (11½ oz) ramen noodles
salted peanuts

PROBABLY THE QUICKEST AND THE MOST COMFORTING NOO DISH YOU'LL EVER MAKE. PERFECT MID-WEEK MUNCH.

01 Add 3 tablespoons of smooth peanut butter, 4 tablespoons of soy sauce, the garlic, 2 spring onions, 2 tablespoons of agave nectar, 3 tablespoons of rice wine vinegar, ½ teaspoon of Szechuan peppercorns and a peeled and grated 5-cm (2-inch) piece of ginger to a blender. Add 1 tablespoon of vegetable oil and 4 tablespoons of water and blitz until very smooth.

02 Get the noodles on (follow the packet instructions).

03 Once the noodles are cooked, drain and add them to a large bowl. Pour your peanut butter sauce over the top and toss everything together.

04 Serve the noodles with some bashed salted peanuts on top, and some chopped spring onion as a garnish.

INGREDIENTS

5 shallots
3 red chillies
paprika
fresh ginger
fresh coriander (cilantro)
kaffir lime leaves
4 garlic cloves
lemongrass purée
400 g (2¼ cups) rice
vegetable oil
750 g (1 lb 10 oz) boneless,
skinless, diced chicken thighs
1 x 400-ml (14-fl oz) tin of
coconut milk
150 g (5½ oz) mange tout
(snow peas)

SACK OFF THE READY-MADE PASTE AND MAKE YOUR OWN. SO MUCH FRESHER, SO MUCH HEALTHIER. GO ON MOB!

01   Curry paste time. Add the shallots, chillies, 3 teaspoons of paprika, a peeled and grated 5-cm (2-inch) piece of ginger, a bunch of coriander stalks, 5 kaffir lime leaves, garlic and 3 heaped teaspoons of lemongrass purée to a blender.

02   Blitz everything until it is smooth.

03   Get the rice on (following the instructions on the packet).

04   In a pan, add a glug of vegetable oil, and then throw in the diced chicken thighs. As it starts to brown, add your curry paste. Cover the meat in it, and fry so the paste starts catching on the bottom of the pan.

05   At this point, pour in the coconut milk, and refill the tin half way and pour that in. Throw in the mange tout. Bring the curry to a boil, and then cook over a medium heat for 10 minutes.

06   When the curry is thick and the chicken is cooked through, remove from the heat. Fold in some fresh coriander leaves and serve on the hot rice. Enjoy!

INGREDIENTS

8 squid (prepared by a
fishmonger)
anchovies in oil
2 garlic cloves
dried chilli flakes
fresh parsley
250 g (9 oz) cherry tomatoes
300 g (10½ oz) giant couscous
capers
Kalamata olives
lemon
olive oil
salt and pepper

**COMFORT IN A DISH,
THIS IS A REALLY EASY,
WARMING SUPPER.
CHARGRILL THE SQUID
SEPARATELY FOR
EXTRA FLAVOUR!**

GRIDDLED SQUID PUTTANESCA WITH GIANT COUSCOUS

01 You will need to buy prepared squid for this recipe. In case you have to prepare it yourself though, first remove the tentacles by pulling them away from the body and set them aside. Remove the shard-like 'quill' from the body. Rinse the inside of the squid. Pull the wing-like flaps from the body and pull away the skin with your fingers. Cut the tentacles just below the eyes and discard the portion above the eyes. Remove the hard 'beak' from the tentacles and the ink sack.

02 Slide a knife inside the tube-shaped squid body, and slice out of one side. You will be left with a nice flat piece of squid. Score the squid in a criss-cross pattern, and then drizzle it in olive oil and season it with salt and pepper.

03 Get a frying pan (skillet) over a medium heat. Add 3 chopped anchovy fillets and 1 tablespoon of anchovy oil (from the tin), chopped garlic, ½ teaspoon of dried chilli flakes and 1 tablespoon of chopped parsley stalks. As the garlic begins to soften (30 seconds), add the tomatoes and 3 tablespoons of water.

04 Get the giant couscous cooking in a separate pan (follow the instructions on the packet).

05 Time to get your squid on. Heat a griddle pan, and then place the squid in the pan, scored-side down. You'll probably have to do this in 2 batches. Press the squid down with a spatula, and cook for 2 minutes on each side. Throw in the tentacles separately – they will take about 4 minutes to cook through.

06 Back to the sauce. The cherry tomatoes should be starting to shrivel. Add 1½ teaspoons of capers and 15 Kalamata olives. Mix everything together, and add a splash more water if needed.

07 Once the squid is cooked, remove it, chop the big pieces in half, and then throw it all into your sauce. Stir it around, and then add 50 ml (3 tablespoons) of the water your couscous is cooking in. Don't worry, this will reduce and you will be left with a delicious rich sauce.

08 Once the sauce has thickened, add some chopped parsley, a good grinding of pepper and a squeeze of lemon juice. Drain your couscous, and load it into 4 bowls. Spoon your squid sauce on top of it, add some more parsley leaves and tuck in!

TOM KHA GAI

INGREDIENTS

1 chicken stock (bouillon) cube
1 x 400-ml (14-fl oz) tin of
coconut milk
lemongrass purée
fish sauce
fresh ginger
1 red chilli
500 g (1 lb 2 oz) diced chicken
breasts
250 g (9 oz) chestnut
mushrooms
1 lime
fresh coriander (cilantro)
salt

01 Add a stock cube to a measuring jug (pitcher) and 750 ml (3 cups) of hot water. Stir and allow the cube to dissolve.

02 Add the stock and the coconut milk to a deep saucepan. Stir the mixture together over a medium heat and when it reaches the boil, turn the heat down to low.

03 Add 1 heaped teaspoon of lemongrass purée, 1½ tablespoons of fish sauce, a peeled, grated 5-cm (2-inch) piece of ginger and a grated chilli. Stir together, and then add the diced chicken breasts and chestnut mushrooms.

04 Squeeze in the juice of a lime, and cook the soup for 8–10 minutes, until the chicken is cooked through. Season with salt, and then serve in bowls with a handful of chopped coriander scattered on top.

A CLASSIC VIETNAMESE SOUP. SO QUICK, SO EASY. SO WARMING. VEGAN MOB – JUST SWAP IN TOFU AND VEGGIE STOCK INSTEAD OF THE CHICKEN STOCK AND FISH SAUCE!

FUSS-FREE
MOB

4

CHICKEN FAJITA PILAF

SERVES 4
40 mins

Louis Berry
25 Reasons

INGREDIENTS

300 g (10 oz) basmati rice
3 (bell) peppers (red, orange
or yellow)
1 red onion
8 skinless, boneless chicken
thighs
smoked paprika
ground cumin
1 lemon
1 chicken stock (bouillon) cube
fresh coriander (cilantro)
black pepper

**ALL THE BEST FLAVOURS
OF A FAJITA IN A NO-FUSS,
ONE-POT PILAF. FOLLOW
STEP 1 CAREFULLY FOR
THE FLUFFIEST PILAF
IN TOWN.**

01 Pour the basmati rice into a pan. Cover with cold water and leave to soak for 10 minutes. After 10 minutes, pour the rice into a sieve (strainer) and rinse thoroughly to drain the starch. This results in a fluffy pilaf. Set the rice aside.

02 Cut the peppers into long strips and finely chop the red onion. Slice the chicken thighs into strips. Add everything into a large, deep-set frying pan (skillet) with a lid. Add 1 heaped teaspoon of smoked paprika and the same of cumin. Grate in the zest of a lemon, season with pepper and mix everything together well.

03 Add a stock cube to a measuring jug (pitcher) and 700 ml (2¾ cups) of hot water. Stir and allow the cube to dissolve.

04 Once the chicken has browned and the peppers are beginning to soften, pour in your rice. Mix it through the chicken and vegetables, and then pour in your chicken stock. Bring it to the boil, then turn it down to a simmer, cover and let it cook for 15 minutes.

05 After 10 minutes, check the pilaf, and give it a stir to make sure nothing is catching on the bottom of the pan.

06 After 15 minutes, turn off the heat and allow the rice to steam, lid on, for 5 minutes. After this, remove the lid and add a large handful of chopped coriander. Squeeze in the juice of half a lemon, fluff up the rice and serve it up!

SERVES 4

1 hr 10 mins

The Four Owls

Defiant

INGREDIENTS

8 boneless chicken thighs
(skin on)
270 g (9½ oz) cherry tomatoes
1 large chorizo sausage
2 red (bell) peppers
1 large ciabatta loaf
dried chilli flakes
fresh basil
1 lemon
pitted green olives
olive oil
salt and pepper

**THE ULTIMATE TRAYBAKE.
THE CRUNCHY CROUTONS,
THE CRISPY CHORIZO, THE
SALTY CHICKEN SKIN, THE
SHRIVELLED TOMATOES.
IT'S ALMOST TOO GOOD
FOR WORDS.**

CRISPY CHICKEN & CHORIZO TRAYBAKE [★]

01   Preheat the oven to 180°C fan (200°C/400°F/Gas Mark 6).

02   Put the chicken thighs in a baking dish, skin-side up. Throw in the cherry tomatoes.

03   Make sure you remove the outer skin from the chorizo. Then chop it into nuggets. Slice the red peppers into chunks. Add both to the baking dish.

04   Tear the ciabatta loaf into chunks and add to the baking dish. Add a pinch of dried chilli flakes. Season with salt and pepper, drizzle over some olive oil and place in the hot oven for 1 hour, mixing everything about halfway through to make sure it all gets coated in the juices.

05   While the pan is in the oven, make your dressing. Add a large handful of chopped basil, the juice of a lemon and 4 tablespoons of olive oil to a jar. Mix it together.

06   Remove the baking dish from the oven 10 minutes before the hour is up and add a large handful of olives. Return to the oven to finish.

07   When the chicken skin and ciabatta chunks are golden and crispy, remove the pan from the oven.

08   Drizzle the dressing over and serve!

ONE-POT VEGGIE TAGINE [V]

INGREDIENTS

2 aubergines (eggplants)
1 butternut squash
butter
1 red onion
2 garlic cloves
ground cumin
ground ginger
ground cinnamon
1 x 400-g (14-oz) tin of plum
tomatoes
1 x 400-g (14-oz) tin of
chickpeas – do not drain!
vegetable stock (bouillon) cube
dried apricots
400 g (2½ cups) couscous
pitted green olives
1 lemon
plain yogurt
fresh coriander (cilantro)
olive oil
salt and pepper

SO EASY TO MAKE USING JUST ONE PAN. THIS IS THE ULTIMATE VEGGIE TAGINE FOR UNDER A TENNER. THE OLIVES REALLY GIVE THE DISH A NICE FRESH KICK AT THE END.

01 Cut the aubergines and butternut squash into cubes.

02 Place the tagine (use an ovenproof casserole if you don't have a tagine) over a medium heat and add a little olive oil and a knob (pat) of butter. Add a finely chopped red onion and chopped garlic cloves and fry until soft. Then add 1 teaspoon of ground cumin and the same amount of both ground ginger and ground cinnamon.

03 Add the cubed aubergines and butternut squash and continue cooking for another 10 minutes, stirring continuously to infuse the aubergines with all the spices and flavours.

04 Next, add the tin of plum tomatoes and tin of chickpeas (and their water), the stock cube, 100 ml (7 tablespoons) of water and 10 dried apricots. Season with salt and pepper, give it a good stir, then place the lid on for 1 hour, or until thick and the aubergine is cooked through. Keep stirring and add water if it needs it.

05 With a few minutes to go, cook the couscous according to the packet instructions. Once ready, fold in 2 tablespoons of chopped green olives.

06 When the tagine is ready, grate in the zest of the lemon and squeeze in the juice. Add a dollop of yogurt for some creaminess, stir through a handful of chopped coriander and tuck in!

INGREDIENTS

20 g (¾ oz) dried porcini
mushrooms
salted butter
1 brown onion
250 g (9 oz) chestnut
mushrooms
400 g (14 oz) orzo pasta
chicken stock (bouillon) cube
Parmesan cheese
fresh parsley
fresh tarragon
salt and pepper

A LITTLE PORCINI REALLY
GOES A LONG WAY HERE.
THIS IS SUCH A WARMING,
COMFORTING DISH. THE
TARRAGON AND PARSLEY
BRING THE KICK.

RICH ONE-PAN MUSHROOM ORZO RISOTTO [V]

01 Soak the dried porcini mushrooms in 120 ml (½ cup) of boiling water.

02 Melt 1 tablespoon of salted butter in a large frying pan (skillet). Add a finely chopped brown onion and cook until soft. Add sliced chestnut mushrooms and cook until they are lightly browned.

03 Add the orzo pasta and stir it around so it is covered with the butter.

04 Add a stock cube to a measuring jug (pitcher) and 675 ml (2¾ cups) of hot water. Stir and allow the cube to dissolve.

05 Add the chicken stock and the water from the porcini mushrooms (but not the mushrooms themselves yet). Bring to the boil over a high heat, then reduce the heat and simmer, stirring often, until the pasta is tender and most of the liquid is absorbed. This should take 12 minutes. If the mixture becomes too thick before the pasta is done, add a little more water.

06 Stir in 100 g (1½ cups) of grated Parmesan. Chop up your soaked porcini mushrooms and stir these in. Add both a handful of chopped parsley and chopped tarragon (reserving some whole leaves of both to garnish) and stir through the dish. Season with salt and pepper.

07 Spoon the risotto into wide bowls and sprinkle with leftover herbage and some extra Parmesan.

INGREDIENTS

1 onion
fresh sage
1 red apple
3 pork sausages
2 carrots
2 parsnips
1 large whole chicken
750 g (1 lb 10 oz) new potatoes
herbes de Provence
125 g (4½ oz) asparagus
olive oil
salt and pepper

YOUR ROAST DINNER ALL IN ONE PAN. STUFFING. ROAST POTATOES. PERFECT CHICKEN. DELICIOUS GRAVY... WHAT MORE COULD YOU WANT?

ONE-PAN SUNDAY ROAST

01 Preheat the oven to 180°C fan (200°C/400°F/Gas Mark 6).

02 Finely chop the brown onion. Chuck it into a frying pan (skillet) with a drizzle of olive oil over a medium heat. Add 5 chopped sage leaves. Season with salt and pepper. Once the onions are soft, remove them from the heat and add them to a bowl along with a grated red apple. Squeeze the meat out of the sausages and mix it in with the onion. Once combined, form into a lump.

03 Get a large metal roasting pan. Chop the carrots and parsnips into strips and line them along the centre of the pan.

04 Take your chicken. Pull up the skin on its backside and stuff the sausage meat inside. Once it is stuffed, set the chicken on top of the carrots and parsnips. Add the new potatoes to the pan. Drizzle olive oil over the chicken and veg, scatter on some herbes de Provence, season with salt and pepper and place the pan in the hot oven for 55 minutes.

05 After 55 minutes, the bird will be nearly cooked. Take it out, and move all the potatoes to one side of the pan. Chop asparagus spears in half and add them to the pan, drizzling them with a little olive oil and seasoning with salt and pepper. The part of the bird with the stuffing inside might be browning a little faster than the rest. If this is the case, simply cover that part with foil.

06 Place the pan back in the oven for 15 more minutes or until the bird is cooked through (insert a skewer into the area of skin between the breast and leg to see if the juices run clear).

07 Once the bird is cooked, remove the pan from the oven. Place the carrots, parsnips, potatoes and asparagus into serving bowls. Scoop the stuffing out of the chicken and place it into a bowl. Remove the chicken from the pan and carve it up.

08 Now for your super quick gravy. Place the roasting pan on the hob over a high heat. Add 4–5 tablespoons of water and with a wooden spatula rub all the sticky bits off the bottom of the pan. Once the bottom of the pan has been rubbed clear, add 150 ml (⅔ cup) water. Keep mixing everything together and reducing the water until you have a nice dark brown gravy. Pour the gravy into a serving jug (pitcher).

09 Make sure everyone gets a bit of everything and tuck in!

INGREDIENTS

1 large chorizo ring
2 red (bell) peppers
2 orange (bell) peppers
2 yellow (bell) peppers
2 brown onions
3 garlic cloves
1 red chilli
fresh coriander (cilantro)
paprika
1 x 400-g (14-oz) tin of
chickpeas – don't drain!
2 x 400-g (14-oz) tins of butter
(lima) beans – don't drain!
olive oil

A SPANISH-INSPIRED STEW THAT WILL WARM YOU TO YOUR CORE. PERFECT FOR WHEN THE WINTER EVENINGS START TO DRAW IN. EVERYTHING IS COOKED IN ONE PAN, SO THERE IS VERY LITTLE WASHING UP. IF YOU'RE A VEGGIE, LEAVE OUT THE CHORIZO AND JUST ADD MORE PAPRIKA.

UNCLE ANDY'S BEAN, PEPPER & CHORIZO STEW [★]

01 Chopping. First remove the outer skin from the chorizo. Then chop it in half and on the angle into slices. Slice the red, orange and yellow peppers into strips. Finely chop the brown onions, garlic, chilli and the leaves from a bunch of coriander.

02 Throw the garlic, chilli and the coriander stalks into a hot, deep-set saucepan, with a healthy glug of olive oil.

03 Once they have softened, add your chorizo.

04 Turn down the heat, so as to allow the fat to render out of the sausages. As the chorizo begins to brown, add the onions. Add some of your chickpea or butter bean tin water to make it more "saucy".

05 Once the onions have sweated off, add the peppers.

06 As the peppers are reducing down, occasionally add splashes of the bean tin water.

07 When the peppers are soft, add 1 heaped teaspoon of paprika and the tin of chickpeas. Allow the chickpeas to soften, and then throw in the butter beans.

08 Cook for another 10 minutes or so.

09 Add three-quarters of your chopped coriander leaves, stir the whole stew together, and then take off the heat.

10 Serve with the remaining coriander on top.

INGREDIENTS

1 brown onion
3 garlic cloves
fresh ginger
1 cauliflower
cumin seeds
dried chilli flakes
garam masala
cardamom pods
350 g (12½ oz) red split lentils
2 x 400-g (14-oz) tins of chopped tomatoes
1 vegetable stock (bouillon) cube
200 g (7 oz) frozen petit pois
300 g (10½ oz) dairy-free coconut yogurt
fresh coriander (cilantro)
olive oil
salt and pepper

A DELICIOUS ONE-POT DHANSAK WITH COOLING CORIANDER COCONUT YOGURT. IT'S GREAT EATEN COLD, TOO, SO MUNCH ON THOSE LEFTOVERS FOR LUNCH THE NEXT DAY!

VEGAN AROMATIC CAULIFLOWER DHANSAK [VG]

01 Finely chop a brown onion. Chop the garlic and a peeled 5-cm (2-inch) piece of ginger. Break a whole cauliflower up into florets. Add them all to a deep-set pan with some olive oil.

02 Add 1 teaspoon of cumin seeds, 1 teaspoon of dried chilli flakes, 2 teaspoons of garam masala and 4 cardamom pods. Mix everything together.

03 Once the onions have softened and the cauliflower is beginning to catch on the pan, add the red split lentils and coat them in the spices.

04 Pour in the tins of chopped tomatoes and keep the tins. Crumble in the veggie stock cube. Season with salt and pepper. Refill the tomato tins with water and pour that in. Stir everything together, bring the dhansak to the boil, and then turn down the heat to a low simmer and cover the pan with a lid.

05 After 20 minutes the lentils should be cooked through and the cauliflower will be ready (still with a bit of crunch).

06 Remove the lid, and pour in the frozen petit pois. Stir them through the dhansak. If it looks a little dry, add a splash more water. Once the peas are cooked through (1–2 minutes), remove the dhansak from the heat and leave to cool for 5 minutes.

07 Meanwhile, make a cooling vegan yogurt sauce. Add the dairy-free coconut yogurt and a large handful of chopped coriander to a bowl. Season with salt and pepper, and then dollop all over the dhansak.

08 Serve it up and tuck in!

FISH & FENNEL STEW

SERVES 4

30 mins (plus defrosting time)

TOPS

Way To Be Loved

INGREDIENTS

400 g (14 oz) frozen cod
1 red onion
1 fennel bulb
3 garlic cloves
fresh parsley
anchovies in oil
dried chilli flakes
white wine (we used Pinot Grigio)
800 g (1 lb 12 oz) passata (strained tomatoes)
1 x 400-g (14-oz) tin of chickpeas
olive oil
salt and pepper

A SUPER-QUICK RICH FISH STEW. USING FROZEN COD IS THE KEY TO KEEPING IT UNDER A TENNER.

01 Take the frozen cod out of the freezer and defrost it.

02 Preheat the oven to 180°C fan (200°C/400°F/Gas Mark 6).

03 Delicately slice up the red onion and fennel bulb (keep the fronds to garnish). Add them to a baking sheet. Drizzle with olive oil and season with salt and pepper. Place the sheet in the hot oven and roast the veg for 20 minutes.

04 Meanwhile, get a saucepan over a medium heat with a splash of anchovy oil from the anchovy tin. Finely slice the garlic and a handful of parsley stalks, and add them to the pan along with 4 chopped anchovies and 1 teaspoon of dried chilli flakes. After 40 seconds, pour in 185 ml (¾ cup) of wine. Once the wine has reduced, add the passata.

05 Bubble the passata down for 5 minutes, and then pour in the chickpeas. Season the stew with salt and pepper. Keep bubbling it down.

06 After 10 minutes the stew should be nice and thick. Chop up your cod into nice big pieces and lob it into the pot. Mix it in. It should take about 5 minutes to cook through.

07 Chop up a handful of parsley leaves. Once the fish is nice and flakey, stir in the parsley and roasted vegetables. Garnish with the leftover fennel fronds and chopped parsley leaves.

H.O.S.H.
Disc Jockey

INGREDIENTS

2 garlic cloves
2 red (bell) peppers
1 brown onion
1 red chilli
500 g (1 lb 2 oz) beef mince
paprika
ground cumin
dried oregano
1 x 400-g (14-oz) tin of kidney
beans
sugar
2 x 400-g (14-oz)s of chopped
tomatoes
400 g (2¼ cups) basmati rice
dark (bittersweet) chocolate
fresh coriander (cilantro)
crème fraîche (sour cream)
olive oil
salt and pepper

**A RICH, CREAMY ONE-POT
CHOCOLATE CHILLI. GET
THE MOB OVER, GET THE
POT ON AND WAIT FOR
THE MAGIC TO HAPPEN!**

CHOCOLATE CHILLI CON CARNE

01   Finely chop your garlic, peppers, brown onion and chilli.

02   Add a splash of olive oil to a large frying pan (skillet) and heat over a medium heat until hot. Add the beef mince and, once it has browned, remove it and add the sliced veg to the pan, along with 2 teaspoons of paprika, 2 teaspoons of cumin and 2 teaspoons of oregano. Stir it in.

03   Once the onions have softened, reintroduce the beef mince, along with the drained kidney beans and 1 heaped teaspoon of sugar. Mix everything together, and then pour in the chopped tomatoes. Bring the chilli to the boil, and then cook, covered, for 30 minutes.

04   Get the rice on (following the instructions on the packet).

05   After 30 minutes, remove the lid from the chilli. It should be nice and thick. At this point, add 60 g (½ cup) of chopped dark chocolate along with a large pinch of salt and pepper. Stir the chocolate in. Once it has melted, stir in a large handful of chopped coriander.

06   Serve the chilli on top of your steaming hot rice, with a nice dollop of crème fraîche on top. Enjoy!

INGREDIENTS

8 boneless chicken thighs
(skin on)
750 g (1 lb 10½ oz) new
potatoes
1 garlic bulb
fresh rosemary
za'atar (Middle Eastern
spice mix)
1 x 500-g (1-lb 2 oz) pot of
Greek yogurt
1 cucumber
fresh mint
1 lemon
olive oil
salt and pepper

**SQUIDGY ROAST NEW
POTATOES, CRISPY
CHICKEN SKIN, BIG
DOLLOPS OF FRESH
TZATZIKI, ALL IN ONE
DISH. BISH, BASH, BOSH.**

ZA'ATAR CHICKEN & NEW POTATO BAKE WITH TZATZIKI

01 Preheat the oven to 180°C fan (200°C/400°F/Gas Mark 6).

02 Place the chicken thighs on a baking dish, skin-side up. Add the new potatoes to the pan. Break up the bulb of garlic and add the cloves, skin on, to the pan. Tear 10–20 rosemary leaves off a bunch of rosemary and throw them in.

03 Add 2 heaped teaspoons of za'atar to the pan. Drizzle with olive oil and season with salt and pepper. Rub the spices and seasoning into the thighs and the potatoes, making sure all the chicken remains skin-side up.

04 Place the pan in the hot oven for 1 hour, making sure you mix it around every 20 minutes or so to ensure even cooking.

05 Tzatziki time. Add the yogurt to a bowl. Grate a cucumber, squeeze out the gratings to remove excess moisture, and add to the bowl. Add a handful of chopped mint, season with salt and pepper, squeeze in the juice of a lemon and mix everything together.

06 After 1 hour the chicken should be crispy and cooked through and the potatoes golden. Remove the pan from the oven and dollop the tzatziki over everything. Serve hot!

Fuss-free **MOB**

5

FLASHY MOB

INGREDIENTS

2 butternut squash
3 garlic cloves
400 g (14 oz) spinach
fresh sage
lasagne sheets
250 g (9 oz) ricotta cheese
Parmesan cheese
Dijon mustard
mozzarella cheese
olive oil
salt and pepper

OOOOOH, THE LAYERS. THE RICH RICOTTA AND BUTTERNUT SQUASH PURÉE. THE SILKY SPINACH AND THE CHEESEY TOP. THIS ONE KNOCKS THE CLASSIC LASAGNE OUT OF THE PARK!

SPINACH, RICOTTA & BUTTERNUT SQUASH LASAGNE [V] [★]

01 Preheat the oven to 180°C fan (200°C/400°F/Gas Mark 6).

02 Halve and de-seed the butternut squash. Whack them in the hot oven for 50 minutes or until soft.

03 Spinach filling time. Finely chop the garlic and throw it in a pan with some olive oil. Cook for 30 seconds, and then drop in the spinach. Once wilted (1 minute), add 6–7 chopped sage leaves. Then, add 125 g (½ cup) of ricotta and 30 g (½ cup) of grated Parmesan. Season with salt and pepper, remove from the heat and set aside.

04 Take your butternuts out of the oven (remove and discard their skins). Place one of them in a blender. Pulse, adding water, until you have a purée. Cube your other butternut squash into bite-sized pieces.

05 In a large bowl, place your butternut purée, your butternut cubes, another 125 g (½ cup) of ricotta, 1 large teaspoon of Dijon mustard and some salt and some pepper. Mix it all together.

06 Assembly time. First, grab a large baking dish. Start with a layer of butternut mixture. Then layer on some lasagne sheets. Then a spinach layer, topped with a good sprinkle of Parmesan. Then more lasagne sheets. Then more butternut squash filling. Then more lasagne sheets. Then, finally, spoon over the remainder of your butternut squash and spinach mixture to make the top layer. Cover with sliced mozzarella and sprinkle the rest of your grated Parmesan over the top. Add a drizzle of olive oil, a good grinding of black pepper, and put into the hot oven for 45 minutes, or until golden brown on top.

07 Check the lasagne 15–20 minutes into cooking – if the top is browning too quickly, just put on some foil, and then remove it 5 minutes from the end. Enjoy!

INGREDIENTS

750 g (1 lb 11 oz) boneless,
skinless chicken thighs

2 leeks

1 brown onion

1 x 200-g (7-oz) pack of smoked
bacon rashers

fresh tarragon

plain (all-purpose) flour

560 ml (1 pint) whole milk

1 x pack of puff pastry

1 egg yolk

Dijon mustard

salt and pepper

olive oil

**THE KING OF THE PIES.
THE TARRAGON MAKES IT.
MANDATORY DOLLOP OF
MUSTARD. YOU HAVE TO
GIVE THIS ONE A GO.**

THE ALMIGHTY MOB CHICKEN PIE [★]

01   Preheat the oven to 180°C fan (200°C/400°F/Gas Mark 6).

02   Dice up the boneless chicken thighs into chunks. Brown them off in a large frying pan (skillet) with some olive oil. Remove the chicken from the pan and set aside. Don't wash up the pan yet.

03   Finely slice the leeks, a brown onion and smoked bacon.

04   Add the bacon to the chicken pan, and fry until crispy. Deglaze the pan with a splash of water, and then add the leeks and onion.

05   Fry until soft, adding a splash of water if the vegetables start catching on the pan.

06   Once soft, reintroduce the chicken (again). Stir it in, and then add a large handful of chopped tarragon. Stir, and then add 2 heaped tablespoons of plain flour. Mix it in, making sure the flour is absorbed by the mixture.

07   Pour in the whole milk, splash by splash. Keep stirring until you have a thick pie filling. Season generously with pepper, stir in 1 teaspoon of Dijon mustard and then remove the pan from the heat.

08   Take a pie dish. Fill it with the filling. Then lay your puff pastry on top. Trim the sides, and brush the pastry with beaten egg yolk. Add a sprinkle of salt, and then place in the hot oven for 30 minutes, or until the pastry is puffed up and golden.

09   Slice your pie up, and serve with a big dollop of Dijon mustard. Enjoy!

Rae & Christian

Happy

INGREDIENTS

400 g (14 oz) pork sausages

balsamic glaze

2 garlic cloves

dried chilli flakes

200 g (7 oz) cherry tomatoes

400 g (14 oz) dried spaghetti

700 g (1 lb 9 oz) passata
(strained tomatoes)

fresh basil

Parmesan cheese

olive oil

salt and pepper

THESE LITTLE PORK MEATBALLS ARE SO EASY TO MAKE, AND THE BALSAMIC GLAZE REALLY BRINGS THE PERFECT SWEETNESS TO THE DISH.

BALSAMIC-GLAZED SPAGHETTI MEATBALLS

01 Take the pork sausages and squeeze the meat out of the skins. Make 3 little balls per sausage.

02 Add the sausages to a frying pan (skillet) with a splash of olive oil. Once they start to brown, add 1½ tablespoons of balsamic glaze. Stir it around. As it starts to caramelize, add your finely chopped garlic, 1 teaspoon of dried chilli flakes and the whole cherry tomatoes.

03 Get the spaghetti on (follow the instructions on the packet).

04 Once the tomatoes start to shrivel, pour in the passata and season the sauce well with salt and pepper.

05 Bubble the sauce down. Once it is nice and thick, add a handful of basil.

06 Drain the spaghetti and then pour it into the sauce. Stir it around, and then serve it up, making sure everyone gets a nice helping of the balsamic-glazed meatballs! Sprinkle Parmesan and a few basil leaves over the top to finish.

SMOKEY PARMIGIANA [V]

SERVES 4

1 hr 30 mins

Mighty Mouse

In Front of Our Friends

INGREDIENTS

4 aubergines (eggplants)
3 garlic cloves
dried oregano
smoked paprika
brown sugar
3 x 400-g (14-oz) tins of
chopped tomatoes
mozzarella cheese
Parmesan cheese
ready-made croutons
olive oil
salt and pepper

A CLASSIC WITH A TWIST. THE SMOKED PAPRIKA BRINGS OUT THE SMOKINESS OF THE AUBERGINES, AND IT WORKS AN ABSOLUTE CHARM. A COLD SLICE OF THE PARM THE NEXT DAY IS SUBLIME.

01   Preheat the oven to 180°C fan (200°C/400°F/Gas Mark 6).

02   Cut the aubergines into thin strips. Place them in a sieve (strainer) and cover them in salt. Leave them in the sieve for 10 minutes. This will draw out the moisture.

03   During this time, get on with your tomato sauce. Finely slice the garlic and add to a large pan with a splash of olive oil. Add 3 teaspoons of dried oregano and 2 teaspoons of smoked paprika.

04   Mix together and, after 30 seconds, add 1½ teaspoons of brown sugar. Mix it in, and once it starts to caramelize, add the tins of tomatoes. Stir everything together, and bubble the sauce down over a medium heat. You need it to be quite thick.

05   Back to the aubergines. Heat a griddle pan. Place the aubergine slices on the pan, and cook for 3–4 minutes on each side until you have nice, clear char marks. Do this for all of the aubergine, setting the ready slices on a plate.

06   Once the tomato sauce has thickened, season with salt and pepper and remove it from the heat.

07   Spoon a layer of smokey tomato sauce into a deep baking dish. Then add a layer of aubergines. And then a layer of sliced mozzarella. Repeat this layering until the dish is full. Finally, top the dish with a layer of mozzarella and 100 g (1½ cups) of grated Parmesan. Crush up 100 g (3½ oz) of croutons and sprinkle them over the top. Add a pinch more dried oregano and put the dish in the hot oven for 40 minutes or until the croutons are crisp and golden, and the cheese is bubbling.

08   Once ready, remove from the oven. I think Parmigiana is best eaten warm but not piping hot, so let it sit for 15 minutes. Then, slice it up and tuck in!

SERVES 4
20 mins (plus defrosting time)

Magic System
1er Gaou

INGREDIENTS

ground turmeric
ground cumin
coriander seeds
3 garlic cloves
fresh ginger
550 g (1 lb 3 oz) frozen white
fish fillets
1 lemon
1 brown onion
4 vine tomatoes
1 red chilli
400 g (2¼ cups) basmati rice
1 x 400-ml (14-fl oz) tin of
coconut milk
fresh coriander (cilantro)
olive oil
salt

**DONE IN 20 MINUTES,
IT'S AN ABSOLUTE
WINNER. THE LEMON
WORKS A TREAT HERE,
BRINGING THE FRESHNESS.
THE PERFECT
MID-WEEK DINNER.**

SOUTH INDIAN-STYLE COCONUT FISH CURRY

01   Prep your spice paste. Add 1 teaspoon of turmeric, 1 teaspoon of cumin, 2½ teaspoons of coriander seeds, garlic and a peeled 5-cm (2-inch) piece of ginger into a blender. Blitz until you have a rough paste.

02   Defrost the white fish fillets then place in a bowl. Grate in the zest and juice of ½ lemon and add a small pinch of turmeric. Mix it all together and cover.

03   Finely chop a brown onion. Fry with a splash of oil in a wide frying pan (skillet) until soft, and then add your spice paste. You want it to be quite dry in the pan – don't be tempted to add more oil. Once the spices start getting toasty, grate the vine tomatoes, discarding the skins, and add them to the pan. Grate the chilli into the pan and mix everything together.

04   Get the rice on (following the instructions on the packet).

05   Once the moisture from the tomatoes has evaporated, add the coconut milk. Stir everything together, and then add your fish, in large bite-sized chunks. Season the curry with salt. The fish should take about 5 minutes to cook perfectly.

06   Once the curry has thickened, throw in a handful of fresh coriander, squeeze in a bit more lemon juice, stir it in and remove from the heat.

07   Serve on top of the hot rice and enjoy!

VEGGIE CURRY FLATBREAD WRAPS [V]

SERVES 4
50 mins

Brassroots
Good Life

INGREDIENTS

1 cauliflower
1 aubergine (eggplant)
1 sweet potato
garam masala
coriander seeds
olive oil
salt

THE FLATBREADS

self-raising (self-rising) flour
300 g (10½ oz) natural yogurt
bicarbonate of soda (baking
soda)
coriander seeds
cardamom pods
fresh coriander (cilantro)

THE RAITA

200 g (7 oz) natural yogurt
1 cucumber
fresh coriander (cilantro) leaves
fresh mint leaves

TO SERVE

flaked (slivered) almonds
mango chutney

01 Preheat the oven to 180°C fan (200°C/400°F/Gas Mark 6).

02 Break up a cauliflower into florets and place it in a baking dish. Roughly chop an aubergine and a sweet potato into cubes and add to the pan. Add 2 teaspoons of garam masala and 2 teaspoons of coriander seeds. Season with salt, drizzle with olive oil and place the dish in the hot oven for 40 minutes.

03 Meanwhile, get on with your flatbreads. Add 350 g (2½ cups) of self-raising flour, 300 g (10½ oz) of yogurt, 2 tablespoons of cold water, a large pinch of salt and 1½ teaspoons of bicarbonate of soda to a bowl. Add 2 teaspoons of coriander seeds, the seeds from 2 cardamom pods and 1 tablespoon of chopped coriander stalks. Mix it together with your hands until you have a smooth dough. Leave it in the bowl to rest for 10 minutes.

04 Toast your flaked almonds and set aside.

05 Get on with your raita. Add 200 g (7 oz) of yogurt to a bowl. Peel three-quarters of a cucumber. Scoop out the seeds. Then finely grate the cucumber. Squeeze the gratings to remove excess moisture, and then add to the yogurt. Add a handful of finely chopped coriander leaves and the same of mint leaves. Season with salt, and then mix. Place in the fridge.

06 Place a frying pan (skillet) over a high heat. Flour a surface and take large, golf ball-sized pieces of your flatbread dough. Roll it out very thinly, and then place in the pan. Toast on each side for 3–4 minutes.

07 Time to load up your flatbreads. Add a large spoonful of raita. Then add a large spoonful of roasted vegetables. Then some flaked almonds. Then some dollops of mango chutney. Then some herb leaves. Then wrap up your flatbread and take an enormous bite and enjoy!

BIG UP TO THE LEGEND THAT IS EMMA FREUD FOR THE INSPIRATION HERE. THESE FLATBREADS ARE SO QUICK AND EASY TO MAKE. IT'S A REALLY FUN DISH FOR A DINNER PARTY!

SERVES 4
4 hrs 10 mins

Terrence Parker
Somethin' Here (Dub Mix)

INGREDIENTS

500 g (1 lb 2 oz) sliced pork
belly
1 red onion
2 garlic cloves
ground cumin
smoked paprika
1–2 bottles of beer
olive oil
salt and pepper

THE SALSA

1 mango
cherry tomatoes
fresh coriander (cilantro)
4 spring onions (scallions)
1 red chilli
1 lime

THE BLACK BEANS

2 garlic cloves
1 x 400-g (14-oz) tin of black
beans

TO SERVE

8 mini tortillas
fresh coriander (cilantro)
1 lime

BEER-BRAISED PORK BELLY TACOS [★]

01 Preheat the oven to 150°C fan (170°C/325°F/Gas Mark 3).

02 Place the pork belly slices in a roasting pan along with a quartered red onion and the whole garlic cloves. Add 2 teaspoons of cumin and 2 teaspoons of smoked paprika. Season with salt and pepper. Pour over 400 ml (14 fl oz) of beer and add enough water to cover the pork.

03 Cover the roasting pan with foil and cook in the hot oven for 4 hours.

04 In the meantime, make your salsa. Chop a mango into cubes and add to a bowl along with a handful of quartered cherry tomatoes, a handful of chopped coriander, chopped spring onions, chopped chilli and the juice of a lime. Add a drizzle of olive oil and season with salt. Mix together and chill in the fridge.

05 After 4 hours, remove the pork from the oven but leave the oven on. Take off the foil and break up the pork with a fork. Place back in the oven for 20 minutes, until most of the liquid has evaporated and you have your dark, sticky pork.

06 Black bean time. Fry the chopped garlic cloves in some olive oil. After 20 seconds, add the black beans but don't throw away the water in the tin. Coat the beans in the garlic and oil, and then mash them up. Add the water from the tin, and reduce down until you have a black bean mush.

07 Once everything is ready, heat up the mini tortillas, add a dollop of black bean mush, then your pork, and then the salsa. Throw on some coriander leaves and squeeze over some lime juice. Heaven in a mouthful!

> **THE MANGO SALSA CUTS THROUGH THE RICH PORK LIKE A DREAM. YOU'VE GOTTA TRY THIS ONE, MOB.**

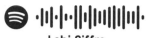
INGREDIENTS

vegetable stock (bouillon)
cubes
1 brown onion
2 garlic cloves
440 g (2¼ cups) arborio rice
frozen petit pois
250 g (9 oz) asparagus spears
salted butter
Parmesan cheese
fresh parsley
fresh mint
1 lemon
olive oil
salt and pepper

**A LIGHT, HERBY, FRESH
RISOTTO. PERFECT
SUMMER MUNCH.
ACCOMPANY WITH A
LARGE GLASS OF COLD
WHITE VINO.**

THE FRESHEST, EASIEST, GREENEST RISOTTO [V]

01 Dissolve 1½ stock cubes in 1.5 litres (quarts) of hot water.

02 Finely dice the brown onion and finely chop the garlic.

03 Add the onion and garlic into a deep pan with a glug of olive oil. Fry until soft, and then pour in the arborio rice. Mix the rice about, coating it in the oil.

04 Keep adding stock, bit by bit. As the rice absorbs the stock, pour in a bit more. Keep beating the rice about with a wooden spoon to release the starches, making it thick and oozy.

05 Five minutes into cooking the rice, add two large handfuls of frozen petit pois into a bowl of boiling water. Chop the asparagus spears into bite-sized pieces, and add them to a separate bowl, covering them with the hot vegetable stock. Leave the vegetables to sit in the boiling water.

06 Back to the risotto. Keep beating and mixing, until the rice is almost done, but still a bit raw in the middle. At this point, drain the asparagus and add it to the risotto. Mix everything together, and then add the petit pois. Keep mixing and adding stock, and then add a large knob of butter. Beat the butter in until it has dissolved and the last of the stock has been absorbed. Season with salt and pepper and remove from the heat.

07 Add some grated Parmesan, a large handful of chopped parsley and a large handful of mint. Mix everything together, squeeze in the juice of ½ lemon, drizzle over some more olive oil, garnish with more chopped parsley and mint, and serve with some Parmesan shavings!

VEGAN TERIYAKI TOFU BURGERS [VG]

SERVES 4
20 mins

Floorplan
Tell You No Lie

THE BURGERS

1 carrot
fresh ginger
5 spring onions (scallions)
1 x 280-g (10-oz) pack of extra
firm tofu (we use The Tofoo
Co.)
dried breadcrumbs
teriyaki sauce
4 burger buns

THE TERIYAKI MAYO

vegan mayonnaise
teriyaki sauce
1 lime

THE ASIAN SLAW

1 carrot
8 radishes
fresh coriander (cilantro)
1 lime
sesame oil

EASY, QUICK AND VEGAN. THE LIP-SMACKING SLAW WORKS PERFECTLY WITH THE TERIYAKI-GLAZED BURGERS.

01 Grate the carrot and a peeled 5-cm (2-inch) piece of ginger, and add along with the spring onions, tofu, 55 g (2 oz) of dried breadcrumbs and 3 tablespoons of teriyaki sauce to a blender. Blitz until everything is bound together and in one solid lump.

02 Remove from the blender and divide into 4 even pieces. Squash into patties, and then brush some extra teriyaki sauce over the top.

03 Heat a non-stick griddle pan. Place the patties in the pan and cook over a medium heat for 4 minutes on each side.

04 While the patties are cooking, halve the brioche burger buns and place under the grill (broiler) so they toast up.

05 Make a quick teriyaki mayo. Add 3 tablespoons of mayonnaise, 1 tablespoon of teriyaki sauce and 2 teaspoons of freshly squeezed lime juice to a bowl and mix.

06 Get on with your Asian slaw. Coarsely grate the carrot and chop the radishes into matchsticks. Add a handful of chopped coriander, the juice of ½ lime and 1 teaspoon of sesame oil. Toss together.

07 Once the burgers are done, remove from the heat. Brush a bit more teriyaki sauce around the edges.

08 Spoon some teriyaki mayo on the bottom half of your toasted bun. Then add your burger. Then pile it with your slaw. Top with the bun and tuck in!

SERVES 4

1 hr 20 mins

Monika

Secret in the Dark
(Juan Maclean edit)

INGREDIENTS

500 g (1 lb 2 oz) spinach
1 brown onion
2 garlic cloves
fresh dill
feta cheese
ricotta cheese
5 eggs
1 x pack filo (phyllo) pastry
sheets
sesame seeds
olive oil
salt and pepper

**IT WILL BLOW YOUR MINDS
HOW EASY IT IS TO MAKE
THIS. THE CRUNCHY FILO,
THE SPINACHY, CHEESEY
FILLING – OH, BABY!**

SHOWSTOPPER CRUNCHY SPANAKOPITA [V]

01 Preheat the oven to 165°C fan (185°C/360°F/Gas Mark 4).

02 Filling time. Wilt the spinach in a frying pan (skillet). Place in a sieve (strainer) and squeeze out the moisture.

03 Add the finely chopped brown onion to a pan with a splash of oil until it softens. Remove from the heat.

04 Add the cooked onion and spinach to a bowl with 2 crushed garlic cloves, a small handful of dill, 200 g (1½ cups) of crumbled feta and 200 g (scant 1 cup) of ricotta. Add 4 eggs. Season with salt and pepper and mix everything together.

05 Pie-building time. Brush some oil on a 25-cm (10-inch) square baking dish. Place 6 sheets of filo pastry on the bottom, brushing each sheet with a little oil when in the dish, and letting them overhang the sides.

06 Ladle in the filling. Place 4 sheets of filo pastry on top. Crimp the pastry sheets together.

07 Brush the top sheet of pastry with a beaten egg yolk and scatter sesame seeds on top.

08 Bake the pie in the hot oven for 1 hour or until the pastry is crisp and golden. Take it out of the oven, cut it up and tuck in!

FAKEAWAY
MOB

6

INGREDIENTS

500 g (3 cups) basmati rice
vegetable stock (bouillon) cube
2 brown onions
3 carrots
4 garlic cloves
curry powder
garam masala
plain (all-purpose) flour
soy sauce
agave nectar
4 aubergines (eggplants)
1 x 400-g (14-oz) tin of
chickpeas
dried breadcrumbs
vegetable oil

AUBERGINES WORK A TREAT IN THIS VEGAN VERSION OF A CLASSIC DISH. YOU CAN ALSO USE SLICES OF BUTTERNUT SQUASH OR SWEET POTATO. GET CREATIVE MOB!

CRUNCHY VEGAN AUBERGINE KATSU [VG]

01   Get the rice on (following the instructions on the packet).

02   Dissolve 1 stock cube in 600 ml (2½ cups) of hot water.

03   Katsu sauce time. Finely slice the onions, carrots and garlic cloves. Fry the vegetables in a large pan with some vegetable oil until they soften. Add 4 teaspoons of curry powder and 1 heaped teaspoon of garam masala. Mix together, and then add 1 tablespoon of flour. Mix that in, and then pour over the prepared vegetable stock.

04   Add 2 tablespoons of soy sauce and 1 tablespoon of agave nectar. Mix together, then allow it to bubble down and thicken.

05   Once the sauce is a thick, pouring consistency, remove it from the heat. Place it in a blender and blitz until smooth. If you don't have a blender, get a masher and mash the sauce, and then pass it through a sieve (strainer).

06   Aubergine time. Cut the aubergines into 2-cm (¾-inch) thick discs. Set aside.

07   Open a tin of chickpeas. It is the liquid we want here, though. Pour it into a bowl, and set the chickpeas aside (you won't need them for this recipe, so keep them for something else). Whisk the chickpea water until it becomes white and fluffy.

08   Lay out a bowl of flour, and a bowl of breadcrumbs. Coat your aubergine in the flour, then cover with the whisked chickpea water and then coat with breadcrumbs.

09   Heat a pan with vegetable oil. Cook the aubergine for 5 minutes on each side, until golden and crispy.

10   Serve the aubergine on a bed of rice, and pour your katsu sauce over the top. Enjoy!

INGREDIENTS

500 g (1 lb 2 oz) lamb mince
ground cumin
fennel seeds
cayenne pepper
dried oregano
1 garlic clove
1 x 500-g (1-lb 2 oz) pot of
Greek yogurt
1 cucumber
2 lemons
1 red onion
fresh parsley
4 large pitta breads
salt and pepper

**SACK OFF THE LOCAL VAN
– THIS BABBY RECIPE IS
THE BUSINESS. HEALTHIER,
TASTIER, CHEAPER – GET
ON IT MOB!**

HOMEMADE DONER KEBAB WITH TZATZIKI & PICKLED ONIONS [★]

01 Preheat the oven to 180°C fan (200°C/400°F/Gas Mark 6).

02 Throw the lamb mince into a bowl. Add 1 teaspoon of cumin, 1 teaspoon of fennel seeds, ½ teaspoon of cayenne pepper, 1 teaspoon of oregano and a grated garlic clove. Season with salt and pepper. Mush everything together.

03 Form the mince into a fat sausage, similar to something like an aubergine (eggplant), and then wrap it tightly in tin foil. Place in the hot oven for 30 minutes.

04 Tzatziki time. Add the Greek yogurt, a grated cucumber (squeeze the gratings to remove excess water), the juice of 1 lemon and salt and pepper. Mix together. Cover, and chill.

05 Pickled onion time. Finely slice a red onion and put into a bowl. Squeeze over the juice of another lemon. Add a pinch of salt. Scrunch the salt and juice into the onions. Leave out until you serve. The acidity of the lemon will take the sharpness out of the onion.

06 After 30 minutes, remove the lamb from the oven. Take off the foil. Set the oven to your grill (broiler) setting and place the lamb under the grill, for 1–2 minutes on each side, so it gets nice and brown. Watch that it doesn't burn.

07 Remove the doner kebab from the grill. Slice it thinly with a sharp knife.

08 Take your onion and add a big handful of fresh parsley to it.

09 Assembly time. Warm the pittas. Dollop in some tzatziki, then add some doner strips. Spoon in some pickled onions, dollop on a bit more tzatziki, and tuck in!

**CHEEKIER THAN NANDOS.
FRESHER THAN NANDOS.
HEALTHIER THAN NANDOS.
CHEAPER THAN NANDOS.
I THINK YOUR CHOICE IS
PRETTY CLEAR.**

THE CHEEKIEST PERI PERI CHICKEN [★]

01 Preheat the oven to 180°C fan (200°C/400°F/Gas Mark 6).

02 Place a whole chicken on a baking sheet. Cover with olive oil. Add 2 teaspoons of smoked paprika and a teaspoon of dried oregano. Rub it in. Place the chicken in the hot oven for 30 minutes.

03 Time to start prepping the sauce. Cut the red peppers and red onion into chunks and chuck them on a baking sheet. Cut a lemon in half. Add the lemon halves, face down, and drizzle olive oil over everything. Place the baking sheet in the oven for 40 minutes.

04 After 30 minutes, remove the chicken, and baste it in the juices. Place it back in the oven for another 30 minutes.

05 When the vegetables and lemon are charred and soft, remove from the oven. Place the onion and the peppers into a blender. Squeeze out the juice from the roasted lemons. Add the chillies, grated garlic cloves, the zest and juice of a fresh lemon, 2 teaspoons of dried oregano and 2 teaspoons of smoked paprika, 1½ tablespoons of red wine vinegar, 1 tablespoon of olive oil and a good pinch of salt and pepper. Blitz until you have a smooth orange sauce.

06 Pour the sauce into a frying pan (skillet), and add 2 bay leaves. Allow the sauce to gently bubble away for a couple of minutes so the bay leaves can infuse.

07 Get the rice on (following the instructions on the packet) and heat up the black beans.

08 While the sauce is getting on, take your chicken out of the oven. Baste it in the juices, and then remove it from the pan. Hack it up roughly.

09 Serve the chicken on a bed of basmati rice and black beans, and pour your sauce over the top. Enjoy, mob. This one's pretty special.

MOB'S MIGHTY MEATBALL MARINARA SUB [★]

SERVES 4
45 mins

Fat Freddy's Drop
Ernie

INGREDIENTS

fresh white bread
whole milk
500 g (1 lb 2 oz) beef mince
500 g (1 lb 2 oz) pork mince
1 brown onion
4 garlic cloves
fresh parsley
ground fennel seeds

01 Preheat the oven to 180°C fan (200°C/400°F/Gas Mark 6).

02 First up, make your meatballs. Start by placing 120 g (4 oz) of crustless white bread in a bowl. Pour enough milk over the bread so it is covered, and then leave to soak and absorb.

03 Add the beef mince, pork mince, a finely diced brown onion, 2 grated garlic cloves, half a bunch of chopped parsley, 2 teaspoons of ground fennel seeds, 3 egg yolks, a good sprinkle of salt and pepper and your milk-soaked bread. Mix everything together with your hands and divide into 12 balls.

04 Place a frying pan (skillet) over a medium–high heat with a good glug of vegetable oil. When the oil it hot, place the balls in the pan. Turn them after 3–4 minutes, and keep turning until brown on all sides. Place in the hot oven for 15–20 minutes until cooked through. Remove the balls and place on a plate.

3 eggs
500 g (1 lb 2 oz) passata
(strained tomatoes)
1 large ciabatta loaf
mozzarella cheese
vegetable oil
salt and pepper

**SACK OFF SUBWAY – THIS
MONSTER IS THE REAL
DEAL. FENNEL SEEDS
BRING THE KICK. THREE
HENCH MEATBALLS EACH!**

05   Wipe out the pan, and then place back on the heat. Fry 2 finely chopped garlic cloves for 1 minute, then add the passata and 250 ml (1 cup) of water. Season with salt and pepper, and then add another half bunch of chopped parsley. Mix everything together, and simmer until thickened.

06   At this point, reintroduce the meatballs to the pan. Turn the balls around in the sauce, and leave to cook over a medium heat for 7 more minutes, bathing the balls regularly.

07   Assembly time. Cut a large ciabatta loaf in half lengthways, and spoon over some of your marinara sauce onto the bottom half. Then add the meatballs, and cover them with the remaining sauce. Lay a thin slice of mozzarella over each ball, sprinkle over a few more ground fennel seeds, and place the sub under a grill (broiler) for 7 minutes or until the cheese has melted. Place the top half under as well so it can toast.

08   When the cheese has melted, remove the sub and place on a board. Scatter some fennel seeds over the cheese to bring real freshness. Take the top half of the loaf and give it a good drizzle of olive oil. Place it back on top of the meatballs, carve it up and enjoy!

THE FALAFEL

500 g (1 lb 2 oz) dried
chickpeas
1 brown onion
3 garlic cloves
fresh coriander (cilantro)
fresh parsley
plain (all-purpose) flour
ground cumin
cayenne pepper
salt and pepper
sunflower oil

THE SALAD

4–6 tomatoes
1 cucumber
fresh mint
fresh parsley
1 lemon
olive oil

TO SERVE

4 large pittas
hummus
pickled green chillies

**CRUNCHY, FRIED FALAFEL
FOR THE INDULGENT
MOB OR BAKED FOR THE
HEALTHIER MOB.**

THE ULTIMATE FALAFEL PITTAS [VG] [★]

01 Pour the dried chickpeas into a bowl, cover with warm water and soak overnight.

02 Preheat the oven to 180°C fan (200°C/400°F/Gas Mark 6).

03 Start with the falafel mix. Add the soaked, dried chickpeas, a chopped brown onion, the garlic cloves, a large handful of coriander, a large handful of parsley, 2 tablespoons of flour, 2 teaspoons of cumin and 1 teaspoon of cayenne pepper into a blender. Season with salt and pepper.

04 Pulse the mixture in a blender. You want the texture to be rough so don't overdo it. Pulsing 3–4 times for 5 seconds each time should do the trick. Check the falafel mixture can stick in a ball. If it is too loose, just add a bit more flour.

05 Make little discs, around 4 cm (1½ inches) wide, and 3 cm (1 inch) deep. Line them up on a sheet of baking paper, and put them in the fridge for 10 minutes to firm up. The mixture should make about 20 discs.

06 Salad time. Chop the tomatoes, peel the cucumber and chop it into chunks, and add to a bowl. Add a handful of chopped mint, a handful of chopped parsley, the juice of a lemon, salt, pepper and a glug of olive oil. Mix.

07 Falafel time. We have designed 2 options. The first is baked falafel – less crunchy but healthier than the fried version. Line a baking sheet with baking paper, and place your falafel on it. Drizzle lightly with olive oil on one side, and then turn over the falafel and drizzle olive oil on the other side. Pat in the oil with your fingers, and then place in the hot oven for 30 minutes, flipping the falafel after 20 minutes.

08 For the fried option, take a wide frying pan (skillet) and heat 1.5 cm (½ inch) of sunflower oil. To check it is hot enough, put in a tiny bit of falafel mixture. When it starts bubbling, it's good to go. Place your falafels in the pan, and cook for 5–6 minutes on each side, or until each side is brown and crisp. Remove the falafels and place on some paper towels. Lay some paper towels on top of them, and pat off the oil.

09 Warm 4 pittas. Layer one side with a good helping of hummus. Spoon in some salad. Take your falafels and break them into the pittas – squeeze in 4–5 discs into each one. Lay some pickled green chillies on top, spoon over a bit more hummus.

THE MARINADE

allspice
ground cinnamon
fresh ginger
4 spring onions (scallions)
4 garlic cloves
fresh thyme
brown sugar
2 Scotch bonnets
vegetable oil
1 kg (2 lbs 3 oz) chicken thighs
and legs

THE JERK GRAVY

1 brown onion
fresh ginger
2 garlic cloves
allspice
ground cinnamon
fresh thyme
1 Scotch bonnet
sugar
plain (all-purpose) flour
1 chicken stock (bouillon) cube
salt

TO SERVE

350 g (12½ oz) basmati rice
1 x 400-g (14-oz) tin of black
beans

FIERY JERK CHICKEN, RICE & PEAS

01 Into a blender add 2 teaspoons of allspice, ½ teaspoon of ground cinnamon, a peeled 5-cm (2-inch) piece of ginger, spring onions, garlic cloves, 3 teaspoons of chopped fresh thyme, 1 tablespoon of brown sugar, the deseeded Scotch bonnets and 1½ tablespoons of vegetable oil. Blitz to smooth.

02 Cover the chicken pieces in the marinade and leave for at least 1 hour. If you have loads of time, it would be best if you left it overnight.

03 While the chicken is marinating, preheat the oven to 180°C fan (200°C/400°F/Gas Mark 6).

04 Once the chicken has marinated, add it to a baking sheet and place in the hot oven for 35–40 minutes.

05 While the chicken is in the oven, get on with your jerk gravy.

06 Dissolve 1 stock cube in 500 ml (2 cups) of hot water.

07 In a frying pan (skillet), add a finely chopped brown onion, 5-cm (2-inch) peeled piece of ginger and garlic, 1½ teaspoons of allspice, ½ teaspoon of ground cinnamon and 2 teaspoons of fresh thyme. Grate in ¼ Scotch bonnet. Add 1 heaped teaspoon of sugar and mix everything together, then add ¾ tablespoon of flour and mix it in again. Then pour in the prepared stock. Stir everything together, season with salt and bubble your gravy down until it is nice and thick.

08 Get the rice on (following the instructions on the packet) and heat up the black beans.

09 When the chicken is cooked through, remove it from the oven. Get a griddle pan on the heat and cook the chicken for 2–3 minutes on each side so it is nice and charred.

10 Serve the chicken on the rice and beans, and pour the jerk gravy over the top. To be eaten with fingers – get messy!

JERK CHICKEN FOR UNDER A TENNER AND SO EASY TO MAKE AT HOME! FIND SCOTCH BONNETS – NORMAL CHILLIES DON'T REALLY CUT IT HERE.

SERVES 4

45 mins

Ratatat

Loud Pipes

INGREDIENTS

butternut squash
olive oil
560 ml (1 pint) whole milk
plain (all-purpose) flour
Dijon mustard
500 g (1 lb 2 oz) macaroni
Cheddar cheese
Parmesan cheese
fresh sage
fresh rosemary
salt and pepper

**THE CREAMIEST MAC 'N'
CHEESE IN THE LAND.
BUTTERNUT SQUASH
BRINGS THE SWEETNESS.
THIS IS AN ABSOLUTE
WORLDY OF AN M'N'C!**

BUTTERNUT MAC & CHEESE [V] [★]

01 Preheat the oven to 180°C fan (200°C/400°F/Gas Mark 6).

02 Peel a butternut squash and cut it into cubes. Place in a roasting pan. Drizzle with olive oil, season with salt and pepper, and roast in the hot oven for 25 minutes (until soft, not browning though).

03 When the butternut is ready, take two-thirds of it and add to a blender. Pour the milk into the blender too, and blitz until smooth.

04 Place a large saucepan on the heat. Add 4 tablespoons of olive oil and 1½ tablespoons of flour. Whisk it together until the flour is absorbed by the oil. At this point, start gradually adding your blended butternut mix, whisking constantly. Once mixed in, add 2 teaspoons of Dijon mustard.

05 Get the macaroni on a separate pan (following the instructions on the packet).

06 Time to grate your cheese. Finely grate 300 g (10½ oz) of Cheddar and 200 g (7 oz) of Parmesan.

07 Into the butternut sauce, add 3 chopped sage leaves and a small handful of chopped rosemary. Mix them in. Then chuck in the remaining one-third of the roasted cubed butternut.

08 Drain your macaroni, and then add it to the butternut squash pan. Mix it all together. Cheese time. Add the cheese, but save enough to sprinkle over the macaroni before going in the oven.

09 Fold the cheese in. Once it has melted, remove the pan from the heat. Pour the macaroni into a baking dish. Sprinkle your leftover cheese on top. Add some sage and rosemary leaves, and a drizzle of olive oil.

10 Place under the grill (broiler) for 3–4 minutes, keeping an eye on it so the cheese doesn't burn.

11 When the cheese is nicely browned, remove the dish from the grill. Dole up and tuck in! Enjoy, mob!

THE BUFFEST BUTTER CHICKEN

SERVES 4
1 hr

Space Echo
Rainbow Power

INGREDIENTS

400 g (2¼ cups) basmati rice
1 onion
garam masala
hot chilli powder
ground turmeric
180 g (6½ oz) tomato purée
(paste)
200 ml (7 fl oz) double (heavy)
cream
low-fat natural yogurt
fresh coriander (cilantro)
olive oil

THE MARINADE

8 boneless, skinless chicken
thighs
low-fat natural yogurt
2 garlic cloves
fresh ginger
garam masala
ground turmeric
1 lime

RICH, CREAMY CHICKEN CURRY, ALL FROM THE COMFORT OF YOUR OWN HOME. IT'S GONNA BLOW YOUR MINDS!

01 Cut the chicken thighs into 5-cm (2-inch) pieces.

02 Marinade the chicken in a bowl with 150 g (¾ cup) of low-fat natural yogurt, crushed garlic cloves, a thumb-sized piece of peeled and grated ginger, 1½ teaspoons of garam masala, ½ teaspoon of turmeric and a squeeze of lime juice, and place in the fridge for 30 minutes–1 hour.

03 Heat some olive oil in a frying pan (skillet) over a medium heat and cook the chicken for 3–4 minutes until cooked. Whack the cooked chicken in a bowl.

04 Get the rice on (following the instructions on the packet).

05 Meanwhile, fry a finely chopped onion with 3 teaspoons of oil until soft.

06 Add 1½ teaspoons of garam masala, ½ teaspoon of hot chilli powder, ½ teaspoon of turmeric, tomato purée and the juice of ½ lime. Add the double cream and low-fat natural yogurt and simmer for 10 minutes until thick.

07 Add the cooked chicken and simmer for 5 minutes.

08 Garnish with a handful of chopped coriander.

09 Serve with the cooked rice and enjoy!

THE MARINADE

8 boneless, skinless chicken
thighs
lemongrass purée
fish sauce
honey
4 garlic cloves
fresh ginger
1 lime

LEMONGRASS, HONEY & GINGER CHICKEN BANH MI

01   Get your chicken marinating. Dice up the chicken thighs and add them to a bowl. Add 3 teaspoons of lemongrass purée, 2 tablespoons of fish sauce, 1½ tablespoons of honey, grated garlic, a peeled and grated 5-cm (2-inch) piece of ginger and the juice of a lime. Season with a pinch of salt, mix everything together and cover with clingfilm (plastic wrap) for 15 minutes.

02   Get on with your pickle. Peel and finely cut the carrots and radishes into matchsticks. Halve and deseed a cucumber and slice thinly on the angle. Add the veg to a bowl with a handful of chopped coriander, 1 tablespoon of white wine vinegar and 1 tablespoon of olive oil. Mix everything together and set aside.

THE PICKLE
2 carrots
10 radishes
1 cucumber
fresh coriander (cilantro)
white wine vinegar
olive oil

TO SERVE
1 large baguette
sriracha mayo
fresh coriander (cilantro)
salt and pepper

03 Place a wide frying pan (skillet) over a medium heat. Add a little oil and then add your chicken when the oil is hot. Cook for 3–4 minutes on each side. Remove from the heat when caramelized on the outside and juicy and tender on the inside.

04 Cut a baguette in half. Add a layer of sriracha mayo. Then a layer of the pickle. Then load it up with the chicken. Then add some coriander leaves and a bit more sriracha mayo. Carve up the banh mi and tuck in!

CLASSIC VIETNAMESE STREET FOOD MADE IN 30 MINUTES. THE ZINGY CHICKEN MARINADE REALLY MAKES THE DISH.

INGREDIENTS

400 g (14 oz) beef steak
cornflour (cornstarch)
vegetable oil
440 g (2½ cups) basmati rice
sesame oil
2 red (bell) peppers
fresh ginger
3 garlic cloves
1 orange
1 red chilli
soy sauce
runny honey
4 spring onions (scallions)

THE CORNFLOUR WORKS PERFECTLY HERE TO GIVE THE BEEF THE BEST CRUNCH. THE ZEST TAKES THE DISH TO A STRAIGHT 10/10.

CRISPY SESAME & ORANGE BEEF STIR FRY

01 Cut the beef steak into thin strips. Place it in a bowl. Add 3 tablespoons of cornflour to the beef, and mix it in until each strip is coated.

02 Add a very big glug of vegetable oil to a wok so that it's about 2 cm (¾ inch) deep. Once the oil is hot, throw in your beef. Do this in batches if you have a small wok. You want each strip to be in full contact with the oil to ensure extra crispiness.

03 Once your beef is brown and crispy, remove from the heat and set aside on some paper towels.

04 Time to get your rice on. Add the basmati rice to a pan using the ratio: 1 part rice, 2 parts water until the water has been fully absorbed. This will ensure fluffy, perfectly cooked rice.

05 Meanwhile, remove the oil from the wok, then place it back on the heat and add 1 tablespoon of sesame oil. Chuck in sliced red peppers. Allow to soften for 3–4 minutes, and then add a peeled, grated 5-cm (2-inch) piece of ginger, garlic cloves, the squeezed juice of an orange and a sliced red chilli.

06 Cook for 3 more minutes and then add the crispy beef back into the wok. Mix everything together, and then add 3 tablespoons of soy sauce, the zest of ½ orange and 1 heaped tablespoon of runny honey. Mix it in and add a small glass of cornflour slurry (mix a heaped teaspoon of cornflour in a small glass of water until it has dissolved) to the wok.

07 Mix everything together, add chopped spring onions, cook for 1 more minute and then remove from the heat.

08 Serve the beef on top of the basmati rice.

INDEX

THANK YOU

First and foremost, I would like to thank the MOB. Without your involvement none of this would be possible. This book is for you.

Next, I would like to thank the head videographer at MOB Kitchen and my best friend Rupert Swan, without whom none of this would be possible.

I would like to thank my mum and dad for their unwavering support, my brothers Joe and Sam for their constant help and advice, and all of my best friends who have been on call at all hours of the day since MOB Kitchen began. You know who you are!

Big shout out to my design team OMSE. James and Briton, the most talented designers in England.

In relation to the book, I would like to thank my amazing team – Liz and Max Haarala Hamilton on photography, Charlie Phillips with the best props about and Alex Gray with the freshest food styling in town. I would like to thank everyone at Pavilion, including Laura Russell and Helen Lewis for bringing the photography team together and Stephanie Milner, Polly Powell and Katie Cowan for supporting the MOB and making this happen. I must also thank my wonderful agent Cara Armstrong at HHB Agency for being my rock and Heather Holden-Brown for her invaluable advice!